MUHLENBERG COLLEGE LIBRARY
ALLENTOWN, PA 18104-5586

GARLAND STUDIES IN

ENTREPRENEURSHIP

edited by
STUART BRUCHEY
UNIVERSITY OF MAINE

A GARLAND SERIES

PROPERTY TAXES AND LOCAL ECONOMIC DEVELOPMENT

PENNSYLVANIA, 1976–1980

DONNA M. KISH-GOODLING

GARLAND PUBLISHING, INC.
NEW YORK & LONDON / 1995

Copyright © 1995 Donna M. Kish-Goodling
All rights reserved

Library of Congress Cataloging-in-Publication Data

Kish-Goodling, Donna M.
Property taxes and local economic development : Pennsylvania, 1976–1980 / Donna M. Kish-Goodling.
      p.   cm. — (Garland studies in entrepreneurship)
Includes bibliographical references and index.
ISBN 0-8153-2173-2 (alk. paper)
    1. Industrial location—Pennsylvania. 2. Pennsylvania—Manufactures—Statistics. 3. Property tax—Pennsylvania.
4. Local taxation—Pennsylvania. I. Title. II. Series.
HC107.P43D55 1995
338.09748—dc20   95-38867

Printed on acid-free, 250-year-life paper
Manufactured in the United States of America

To

Jeff, Megan

and

Matthew

Contents

List of Tables

List of Figures

Acknowledgments

I would like to express my gratitude to Thomas Hyclak, not only for his patience and dedication in reviewing many versions of this study, but also for his work in obtaining a grant from the Small Business Development Center of Lehigh University to purchase the data on firm births. J. R. Aronson, Vincent Munley, and Mary Murphy provided helpful suggestions and editorial assistance. I also received helpful comments from two anonymous referees.

Financial assistance for this project was provided by a fellowship from Lehigh University and full-time employment at Muhlenberg College. I am forever grateful to my colleague and close friend, Elizabeth Patch, for informing Garland Publishing, Inc. of my manuscript. I thank Stuart Bruchey for reviewing and recommending my study for publication to Garland.

I appreciate the moral support and department resources my Department Head, George Heitmann, extended during the final stages of producing a manuscript. I warmly thank my secretary, Anitra Witkowski, for her daily encouragement, friendship, and diligence in producing a camera-ready copy. I also thank Robert McKenzie, my editor. He was always a source of helpful hints and recommendations.

I am grateful to my parents, John and Rose Mary Kish, for their daily babysitting and emotional support throughout the long duration of this project. For their help in running errands and xeroxing, I thank my brother, John Kish, and my stepdaughter, Megan Goodling. I am thankful I had my son, Matthew, to fill the years this project entailed with his ability to make life joyous.

Finally, I want to extend a special thanks to my husband, Jeffrey Goodling, for his valuable computer expertise, financial support, and personal sacrifice. His unrelenting encouragement and inspiration motivated me to accomplish this dream while I taught full-time, in spite of the demands I faced from the conception, birth, and toddlerhood of our wonderful son, Matthew.

Property Taxes and Local Economic Development

I

Do Property Taxes Matter?

INTRODUCTION

According to Tiebout, mobile residents can "vote with their feet" among an assortment of communities competing with different tax-expenditure budgets.[1] Firms may also be attracted to or repelled from communities for a similar rationale. This is an important consideration for local policy makers. Do increases in local tax rates have a negative impact on local economic development activity?

Since the 1950s, researchers have been debating whether or not increases in taxes "drive industry out."[2] Studies using surveys as well as statistical methods have been undertaken using a vast array of different models, data, regions, time frames, and geographic scopes. Some studies focus on general business taxes, including income and real estate. Others also investigate personal income taxes. Overall, however, the results are not conclusive.

Property taxes have traditionally been the principal revenue source for municipalities. The property tax is an important economic variable which is under the control of local public officials. In spite of a plethora of empirical research in this area, results have not yet settled the debate on whether or not property taxes affect local economic development.

THE HYPOTHESIS

This study is an investigation of the effect of property tax rate differentials on the birth of firms in the 67 counties of Pennsylvania from 1976-1980. The hypothesis is that local property taxes influence the location decisions of "footloose" firms—that is—those which are

3

not required to locate near their market or their resource base. Traditionally, national manufacturing firms have been considered more footloose than service or nonmanufacturing firms which typically require close proximity to their markets. However, technological changes, in particular, telecommunications advancements, have permitted some nonmanufacturing firms to locate farther from their markets than in the past. Therefore, it is possible that certain nonmanufacturing industries are "footloose."

General location theory can be condensed to state that a firm's location decision depends on a vector of market and cost characteristics that vary by location and by sector or industry. The market variables may include per capita income and population density. Cost factors would include the supply and price of unskilled, skilled and managerial labor; the cost of capital; the price and availability of land; access to transportation facilities; agglomeration economies; energy prices; and the quality and size of a location's infrastructure.[3]

Local tax differentials can also affect the location decision. Property taxes enter the framework because they may be capitalized as part of the price of land (and sometimes buildings). Within a small region they could explain much of the variation in the price of this factor. However, if taxes on capital are not fully capitalized into the price of land or cannot be fully shifted to consumers, then the burden of the tax falls on the owners of capital through lower after-tax profits. In cases where a firm is successful in shifting the tax onto consumers, then the firm's profits could be adversely affected if it faces an elastic demand for its product, since higher prices would then lead to less total revenue. Therefore, tax differentials can be a pivotal factor if all other site characteristics are equal.[4]

The effect of property tax differentials may not always be negative. Property taxes in certain instances may simply reflect the level of local public services. Firms may be willing to pay higher taxes in return for better fiscal benefits such as police and fire protection, water systems, and access to high-quality educational facilities for their employees' families. As a result, tax differentials must be evaluated against differences in fiscal expenditures.

An additional factor in analyzing the effect of property tax differentials on firm location decisions is the disparity between the highest and lowest property tax rate charged by the various school districts within a particular county. It is possible that firms would be attracted to locate in the lowest tax rate school district within a county if higher tax rate school districts nearby produce positive externalities, such as better quality school districts for their employees to reside in or better pools of skilled labor to hire. Therefore, a wide range or difference between the highest and lowest tax rates may lead to more firm births.

One of the shortcomings of locational theory is its disregard for noneconomic factors. Wasylenko points out that "interview data often indicate that personal factors or historical accident, such as the location of the firm near the birthplace of its founder, are determining factors, especially among smaller firms."[5] Preferences for climate, urban versus rural living, and commuting distance are some of the other variables that can enter an entrepreneur's utility function. One would expect these factors to be more influential for a small business than for a large corporation. However, moving costs of large fixed capital and the cost of obtaining complete information on new locations are more likely to lead large firms to locate in less than the theoretically optimal location.

FOCUS OF EMPIRICAL WORK

This analysis is an intercounty study of the factors that influenced the births of manufacturing and nonmanufacturing firms which occurred in the state of Pennsylvania during 1976-1980. The primary emphasis is on whether or not property tax rate differentials have a statistically significant effect on firm births at the county level. Manufacturing firms presumably have a higher degree of footlooseness. Therefore the manufacturing sector is analyzed separately from nonmanufacturing firm births.

There are 3,136 different taxing jurisdictions that levy a property tax in Pennsylvania. They include 505 school districts, 2,564 municipal governments and 67 county governments. Studies examining the effects of property tax rate differentials aggregate these three property tax rates. This study analyzes the effects of school property tax rates separately from municipal and county property tax rates. In addition, the disparity between the highest and the lowest property tax rate in a county is empirically tested to see if it influences firm location decisions.

THE FOCUS ON FIRM BIRTHS

A firm birth is defined as an establishment that Dun & Bradstreet finds in existence in 1980 which did not exist in 1976. We assume that a firm birth is the manifestation of a location decision of a new business during the time period of 1976-1980. This period was selected because the macroeconomic climate was relatively conducive to business growth. The average annual growth rate of real GNP was 4.35%[6] with an average unemployment rate of 6.7%.[7] In Pennsylvania, the average unemployment rate was 7.4%.[8] The average annual growth rate of nominal GSP (Gross State Product) was 8.6%.[9] The change in the GNP deflator averaged 7.66%[10] for the period, so even though the rate of real growth of the state's economy was less than the growth of real GNP, the average growth rate of real GSP was positive.

Firm births were selected as the focal point for this study instead of new employment because property taxes affect the location of a firm, but not necessarily the number of jobs created. Wasylenko points out that research should be focused on firm births because Birch (1979) and Birch et al (1979) found that employment growth occurred in regions, and in jurisdictions within a region, because of differential numbers of firm births and on-site expansions.[11] Bartik states that studies relying on aggregate employment data can only examine the net effect of decisions regarding births and deaths, expansions, and relocations.[12]

There are several other researchers who have chosen firm births as the dependent variable over employment. For example, Carlton's seminal article published in 1979 uses births as the dependent variable, but his time frames are 1967-1971 and 1972-1975. Howland's 1985 study examines firm births between 1975 and 1982 in only two industries for the 106 counties in Maryland, New Jersey, Virginia and the District of Columbia. Reynolds (1994) analyzes firm birth rates for 1984-86 and 1986-88 in 382 United States labor markets because "new firms not only provide jobs during the founding process, those with growth create additional jobs during their expansion."[13] Papke concludes in her June 1991 study analyzing manufacturing firm births that "the establishment is the appropriate unit at which to explore" tax differentials.[14]

ADVANTAGES OVER PREVIOUS WORK

The geographic scope of this study is confined to one state, with data collected by county. As a result, this study has several advantages over previous work. First, multi-state studies mix together states which have different property tax rules, leading to measurement problems and improper comparisons. This study is based on data collected on local governments under the jurisdiction of one state government in which the millage rates for property taxes are uniformly applied to both residential and commercial/industrial property.

A second advantage is that this study examines the intrajurisdictional distribution of property tax rates. Interstate studies which choose to use average rates suffer from too much aggregation of property tax rates. Within a county or metropolitan area, there is a distribution of taxing jurisdictions and many overlap. In the state of Pennsylvania there are 3,136 different taxing jurisdictions that levy a property tax. They consist of 505 school districts, 2,564 municipal governments and 67 county governments. Interstate studies average the property tax rate across all the taxing jurisdictions. This study will analyze them separately. It is possible that a state with a high average property tax rate could contain very low tax rate jurisdictions within it. Since all studies (including those on a metropolitan level) involve some level of aggregation, the distribution of property tax rates is ignored. My approach will take this important factor into consideration by including not only the average effective property tax rate, but also the range between the highest and the lowest property tax rate in the county. The range (or difference) will be used to analyze the effect of the dispersion of the rates.

Thirdly, the state of Pennsylvania has several favorable characteristics regarding its administration of the property tax. The most important is that, with the exception of 15 municipalities, local jurisdictions use a uniform or non-classified tax system. According to the ACIR, a classified tax system is undesirable, especially if it entails different assessment levels "because it increases the abuse of the assessment process and appears to make the assessor part of the tax-setting process."[15] The state does not use the general property tax for state purposes. Except for intangibles, personal property and business inventories are not taxed. Statutory restrictions on local power to raise property tax revenue is organized by county classes or size.[16]

Even though assessment is done at the county level, the millage rate varies substantially within a county. In order to compare one county with another, the Commonwealth of Pennsylvania publishes equalized millage rates and market valuations for each borough, city, and township, by county. The average equalized millage rate for the county's school taxes is a weighted average. Since the state calculates these equalized millage rates, it is possible to more closely examine the real burden of the tax, thereby avoiding ad hoc calculations and assumptions. Moreover, the county's highest and lowest equalized millage rates can also be included in the model. These will be used to pinpoint high average tax rate counties containing a large dispersion of millage rates. Municipal property taxes will be handled in a similar fashion.

In regards to assessment practices, a study by Ebel and Ortbal comparing property tax relief programs across states found that Pennsylvania was one of the cleanest states concerning circuit breakers, homestead exemptions or credits, and residential deferrals.[17] Widespread use of property tax relief programs would lead to a discrepancy between the stated millage rates and the effective millage rates. Therefore, the absence of these programs in the state of Pennsylvania means the published millage rates are good estimates of the effective millage rates.

Another advantage to using the state of Pennsylvania is that it contains both highly urbanized and extremely rural regions. Pennsylvania is a big state in terms of population. In 1980, it ranked as the fourth largest state in total population[18] and the ninth largest in terms of population density (as measured by persons per square mile.)[19] Seventy percent of the state's population lives in urban areas.[20] Since 74% of the entire American population is urbanized,[21] Pennsylvania has an urban versus rural population mix typical of the United States in general. It also contains a great deal of variation in community size and local economies. Some are expanding while others are contracting.

Since this analysis is for only one state, state taxes can be ignored. Secondly, several other variables, such as degree of unionization, climate, and energy costs found to be important in interstate studies can be excluded. We can presume that the climate throughout the state is homogeneous to the extent that firms would not see significant differences in energy costs.[22] Since Pennsylvania is considered a highly unionized state, even if a county is not widely unionized, we shall assume that there are spillover effects into the nonunion sector. That is, nonunion firms are forced to pay wages close to the union rate due to the potential threat of unionization.

CONTRIBUTION TO THE LITERATURE

This study is an intrastate, intercounty investigation of the effect of property tax rate differentials on local economic development. Based on the literature reviewed in the next chapter, it is the only study which analyzes the separate effects of property tax rates of school districts, municipalities, and county governments, rather than an aggregated effect of them. This study dissects the impact of each of the real estate taxes levied by different and overlapping jurisdictions on firm births. School real estate taxes are examined separately from municipal and county property taxes. This is a major departure from the way property tax rates are included in models throughout the literature.

Finally, studies which include property tax rates in their models do so on an averaged and aggregated basis. This study develops and investigates an augmented model that includes a component to control for the variation of local property tax rates within an individual county. A footloose nascent firm has a choice. It can locate in a community which has very low school and municipal property tax rates, even if the average tax rates for the county are very high. This study tests the hypothesis of whether or not property tax rate differentials are a statistically significant factor in the location of emerging firms.

NOTES

1. C.M. Tiebout, "A Pure Theory of Local Expenditures," *Journal of Political Economy*, vol. 64 (1956).

2. John F. Due, "Studies of State-Local Tax Influences on Location of Industry." *National Tax Journal* (June 1961): 163.

3. Michael Wasylenko, "The Location of Firms: The Role of Taxes and Fiscal Incentives" in *Urban Government Finance: Emerging Trends* edited by Roy Bahl (Beverly Hills: Sage Publications 1981), p. 158.

4. Ibid., 159.

5. Ibid.

6. *Business Conditions Digest* 26, no. 10 (Oct. 1986): 97.

7. Ibid., No. 4 (Apr. 1986): 97.

8. Commonwealth of Pennsylvania, Department of Labor and Industry, *Pennsylvania Total Civilian Labor Force, Unemployment and Employment, Industry Employment by Establishment* 1970-1983, May 1984.

9. U.S. Dept. of Commerce, *Survey of Current Business* 71, no. 12 (Dec. 1991): 47.

10. *Business Conditions Digest* 29, no. 11 (Nov. 1989): 102.

11. Michael Wasylenko, "The Location of Firms: The Role of Taxes and Fiscal Incentives," in *Urban Government Finance* edited by Roy Bahl (Beverly Hills: Sage Publications, 1981), 187.

12. Timothy J. Bartik, "Business Location Decisions in the United States: Estimates of the Effects of Unionization, Taxes, and

Other Characteristics of States," *Journal of Business & Economic Statistics* 3, no. 1 (January 1985): 15.

13. Paul Reynolds, "Autonomous Firm Dynamics and Economic Growth in the United States, 1986-1990, *Regional Studies* 28, no. 4 (July 1994): 429-442.

14. Leslie E. Papke, "Interstate Business Tax Differentials and New Firm Location" *Journal of Public Economics* 45 (June 1991): 65.

15. ACIR, *The Property Tax: Reform or Relief? A Legislator's Guide*, (Washington, DC: ACIR, 1973).

16. ACIR, *The Role of the States in Strengthening the Property Tax*, vol. 2, June 1963, Y3.AD9/8: 2T19/9/v.2 p. 142.

17. Robert D. Ebel and James Ortbal, "Direct Residential Property Tax Relief," *Intergovernmental Perspective* 15, no. 2 (Spring 1989): 11.

18. US Dept of Commerce. *1980 Census of Population: Characteristics of the Population - Number of Inhabitants United States Summary*. Chapter A, Part 1. PC80-1-A1. Bureau of the Census. April 1983, C3.223/5:980/A1 #159-C-52. p. 1-17.

19. Ibid, p. 1-20.

20. Ibid, p. 1-52.

21. Ibid, p. 1-49.

22. Including energy costs is important in interstate studies because there is a wide difference between the state average temperature in Texas versus Maine. However, in a single state, one would not expect a large variation in the average annual temperatures between different counties. According to the *1974 Pennsylvania Statistical Abstract*, the average annual temperature in the state ranged from a low of 38.37 degrees in Butler County in the southwest to 60.16 degrees in Lebanon County in the southeast. The average

annual temperature for the state was 49.65 degrees with a median temperature of 49.6 degrees. The climate throughout the state consists of four distinct seasons.

II

Survey of Literature

INTRODUCTION

The scope of this chapter is confined to papers which examine how property taxes and other fiscal variables affect the location decisions of firms. There is a large body of literature which analyzes tax incidence and efficiency. These topics are not included.

The first section of the chapter is a brief summary of location theory. It is the underlying basis of public finance-focused location studies in the literature. The vast number of papers described in the rest of the chapter are organized in loose chronological order until 1979 when Carlton's seminal work was published. The post-Carlton studies are then discussed in terms of three major classifications. Interstate and intermetropolitan studies will be summarized first, followed by intrametropolitan studies.

LOCATION THEORY

Location theory models analyze optimal firm locational decisions through emphasis on a firm's production costs and its market demand. Early locational theorists such as Weber (1929), Hotelling (1929), Losch (1954), and Greenhut (1956), provided the basic ingredients to a theoretical framework. Weber's least-cost theory of manufacturing firms centered on selecting a geographic area where transportation costs of inputs and outputs are minimized. Only then were labor costs and agglomeration economies considered in selecting a final site. In contrast, Losch's theory concentrated on finding a location where profits are maximized, which is not necessarily where transportation costs or wages are the lowest. Greenhut extended the model by noting that locational variables differ by industry because markets and production inputs vary accordingly. For example, some industries require technical workers and therefore their location decisions may be influenced by the availability of this input.[1]

In general, the location theory literature can be condensed to state that a firm's location decision depends on a vector of market and cost characteristics that vary by location and by industry. The market variables may include per capita income and population density. Cost factors would include the supply and price of unskilled, skilled and managerial labor; the cost of capital; the price and availability of land; transportation costs; agglomeration economies; energy prices; and the extent of a location's infrastructure.[2]

EARLY FISCAL STUDIES

Local tax differentials can also affect the location decision. Property taxes may be capitalized in the price of land (and sometimes buildings). Within a small region they could explain much of the variation in the price of land. However, if taxes on capital cannot be capitalized into the price of land or cannot be shifted onto consumers, then the burden of the tax falls on the owners of capital through lower after-tax profits. In cases where a firm is successful in shifting the tax onto consumers, then the firm's profits could be adversely affected if it faces elastic demand for its product, since higher prices lead to less total revenue. Therefore, tax differentials can be a pivotal factor if all other site characteristics are equal.[3]

John F. Due's 1961 article surveys the early studies addressing the question of whether or not state and local taxes affect the location decision of firms. He reviews the findings of the major statistical studies of relative tax burdens and growth rates. They include Bloom (1955), Thompson and Mattila (1959), Campbell (1958), Commonwealth of Pennsylvania Tax Study Committee (1955), Yntema (1959), Floyd (1959), and several others published between 1950 and 1960. Due concludes that "relatively high business tax levels do not have the disastrous effects often claimed for them."[4] He qualifies his remarks with an ancillary conclusion:

However, without doubt, in some instances the tax element plays the deciding role in determining the optimum location, since other factors balance. This is most likely to be the case in the selection of the precise site in a metropolitan area (property taxes being the ones of chief concern), or when a suitable area for site location straddles a state border. But state and local taxes represent such a small percentage of total costs that the cases in which they are controlling cannot be very significant.[5]

His third major conclusion is that a state's tax climate factor, or the general business reputation or climate of the state, may influence a location decision, but is unlikely to affect a significant portion of locating firms. Beyond his major conclusions, he points out the importance of public services and their role in local taxation. If firms only view taxes negatively without consideration of the positive benefits of the public services they provide, inefficient allocation of resources can result. In retrospect, his argument is insightful for setting the direction of empirical work following the publication of his article. Up to this point, public services or expenditures were ignored in location decision studies analyzing the effects of taxes.

Moriarty (1980) outlines two other early literature survey articles in which Morgan (1964) reviewed seventeen studies that used questionnaires and Stinson (1968) reviewed twenty-six studies of various types published between 1955 and 1966. Moriarty also refers to a study by the ACIR[6] published in 1967. In all instances, Moriarty concludes that there is little evidence that tax effects are an important factor for locating firms.[7]

MAJOR EMPIRICAL STUDIES DURING THE EARLY 1970s

Three studies published in the early 1970s entailed a greater level of sophistication in both the models and the data employed than the multitude of studies from the prior decade.

Fox's 1973 study of the Cleveland and Cincinnati areas provides a model of industrial investment in which the per capita increase in industrial tax base from 1964-69 is the dependent variable. Independent variables of interest include the statutory property tax rate, price of land, percentage of vacant land, and per capita safety expenditures as a measure of local amenities. Access variables include access to interstate highways, population density, the distance to the city center, and the percentage of real property base that is industrial.

The estimates for the Cleveland area produce a tax rate coefficient that is negative and statistically significant. However, the signs of the coefficients for vacant land and highway accessibility are negative—contrary to what is expected. Oakland considers this result to be "suggestive of an underlying weakness in the model."[8] The results for the Cincinnati region are weaker in the sense that the property tax rate coefficient is positive and is not statistically significant. The other independent variables either have incorrect signs or are not statistically significant.

Oakland's analysis of Fox's work attributes the poor performance of the model for Cincinnati to the fact that Fox excludes the Kentucky portion of the MSA and the property tax differentials are narrower in Cincinnati than they are in Cleveland. Even though the Cincinnati estimates weaken Fox's argument that local taxes affect location decisions, his study is important because it is one of the first to show a negative and statistically significant coefficient on a local tax variable. Fox's model for the Cleveland area provides results that the property tax rate has a statistically significant negative effect on the per capita increase in the industrial tax base.

Schmenner's 1973 dissertation and later empirical work published in 1975, 1978, and his book in 1982 are often cited as providing evidence that tax effects are not major determinants of firm location. The unpublished and later revised dissertation is more comprehensive than the Fox study. It not only analyzes property tax differentials, but also includes local income tax differentials as well. His study includes the municipalities of four metropolitan statistical areas (MSAs) for two separate time periods—1967-69 and 1969-71. The MSAs are Cleveland, Cincinnati area, Kansas City, and Minneapolis-St. Paul. Schmenner estimates different regression equations with four dependent variables: manufacturing employment levels and their percentage changes, and the number of manufacturing establishments and their percentage changes. He produces estimates separately for each MSA as well as pooled estimates for the four areas.

The results do not show a statistically significant relationship between tax differentials and the level of employment or the number of establishments. In many cases the signs are wrong. The only exception is for the Cleveland area, where the local income tax rates showed a statistically significant and negative relationship with employment levels. However, since only seventeen out of fifty-seven municipalities have a different income tax rate than Cleveland, Oakland's often-cited critique of Schmenner's work dismisses this finding as a fluke, "probably reflecting rounding errors."[9]

Schmenner's estimates for the models using percentage changes as dependent variables, however, give more interesting results. One of Schmenner's major conclusions is that income tax differentials are important location determinants, but property tax differentials are not. In other words, he finds a statistically significant and negative relationship between income taxes and the percentage change in the number of manufacturing establishments. Schmenner's results are the reverse when the percentage change in employment is the dependent variable. When the four regions are aggregated, the property tax is statistically significant and negatively affects the percentage change in employment levels. The income tax is not statistically significant. For individual MSAs, however, the property tax variable does not reveal any statistical significance, thereby signaling regional differentials are not important.

In his critique of Schmenner's work, Oakland disagrees with Schmenner's conclusion that income tax differentials negatively affect the percentage change of manufacturing establishments. First, in regards to the regressions in which the dependent variable is the percentage change in the number of establishments, the R^2 are very low at .25 or below. Secondly, the negative and statistically significant relationship between income taxes and the change in establishments only occurs when the four MSAs are aggregated. However, analysis of the income tax data does not support this finding. The problem with the Cleveland income tax was already noted—less than one third of the municipalities in the Cleveland MSA have an income tax. In addition, Minneapolis-St.Paul did not have an income tax for the period. In the Kansas City MSA, only the city of Kansas City levies the tax, the suburbs do not. Cincinnati is the only area that had sufficient variation in the local income tax to have any explanatory value. However, in the Cincinnati regression, the variable is statistically insignificant. Therefore, Oakland questions Schmenner's conclusion that income tax differentials negatively affect the percentage change in the number of manufacturing establishments.

Overall, Schmenner's work is a milestone because of its scope and controversial results. It was a catalyst for future researchers, including Schmenner himself. On balance, the results of this study and extensions of it he published in 1975, 1978, and later, in his book in 1982, are generally cited as evidence that tax differentials are not important in intrametropolitan location decisions. In particular, property taxes and local income taxes are not powerful factors in explaining manufacturing employment levels, the number of manufacturing establishments or the percentages changes in either of these variables.

Additional important empirical investigations of firm location factors include both Fischel's 1974 Ph.D. dissertation and his 1975 publication. They are highly regarded because they provide supply-side considerations to location theory. Fischel's extension of the theory focuses on the quality of a community's environment as a function of the business firms that locate within it. Firms are assumed to contribute to a community's basket of public goods through the property taxes they pay. The tradeoff is the environmental costs incurred by these businesses in terms of the pollution they produce and the other environmental impacts they impose on a community's quality of life. Therefore, a community's demand for firms is based on maximizing the welfare of its citizen's tastes for net fiscal benefits from a broader tax base subject to the environmental costs new firms may inflict. Communities which prefer higher quality environments will presumably charge firms higher property taxes to compensate for negative environmental effects. At the extreme, some communities will "zone out" polluting firms.

Fischel tested his hypothesis by using data from 54 suburban communities in Bergen County in northern New Jersey for 1970. To determine if fiscal benefits exist for localities that admit (do not zone out) businesses, Fischel regressed household property taxes against a vector of independent variables. He also regressed school taxes per pupil against a similar set of independent variables. His results indicate that 70% of all commercial and 52% of all industrial property tax payments benefit residents either by lowering residential taxes or by increasing educational expenditures.[10]

Fischel's work is a contribution to the development of location theory models because it provides evidence that fiscal benefits are important location factors to consider in addition to local taxes. However, the effect of fiscal benefits on firm location decisions is not clear from Fischel's work. His regressions are focused on the relationship between a jurisdiction's median income and the amount of industrial and commercial property there is in the jurisdiction. His hypothesis is that higher median income communities can afford better environmental quality and will therefore zone less land for commercial and industrial use. His results indicate that higher income communities have more commercial (retail outlet) firms, whereas lower income communities have more industrial establishments. These findings may be interpreted as an indication that commercial firms are viewed as less destructive environmentally, and therefore higher income communities zone out "noxious" industrial firms.[11] However, Wasylenko points out that Fischel's analysis leaves open the question whether higher income communities supply fewer sites to industrial firms (zone out), or whether industrial firms demand sites in low income communities.[12]

On balance, the major empirical studies produced in the early 1970s were predominantly intrametropolitan studies that did not provide conclusive evidence that local taxes impact the ultimate location choice of new firms. What distinguishes them from the studies that pre-date them is the heightened level of statistical methodologies used. Based on the mixed results of these papers, future researchers were motivated to investigate new econometric models with larger data sets and different measures of firm location decisions.

CARLTON'S WORK

Carlton's publication in 1979 is one of the most widely cited studies in location empirical analysis. It marks a turning point in terms of the rigor of econometric location studies published after 1979.

Using Dun and Bradstreet data, Carlton estimates the probability of new firm births across MSAs for three manufacturing industries during 1967, 1971, 1972 and 1975. The model is a conditional logit using a Poisson distribution of the number of firm births per MSA of four-digit SIC industries for plastic products, electronic transmitting equipment, and electronic components. The explanatory variables include energy costs, wages, agglomeration effects, business climate, property taxes, corporate income taxes, and individual income taxes.

Carlton's results indicate that firm births are responsive to wages, energy costs and agglomeration effects. The coefficients for most of the tax variables are not negative, nor are they statistically significant. The exception is the corporate income tax coefficient which is positive and significant in two of the regressions.

In extended work published in 1983, Carlton analyzes branch plants and employment instead of births. Industries from three different four digit SIC codes were examined using data aggregated to the MSA level for the years 1967-1971. Only the MSAs for which data was available for the SIC codes chosen are included.[13] The property tax variable is $1 + pt$ where pt is the effective property tax. Carlton's explanation for this variable is based on the "approximation that the cost of capital rises linearly with pt".[14] A weighted average of the state personal and corporate income tax rate is used as the state tax variable in the form of 1 - state tax rate, based on the rationale that profits will decline linearly as the state tax increases.[15] The results are similar to the 1979 study. Agglomeration economies are a strong positive factor for branch plants, but taxes are not. The tax variables are often the wrong sign and always statistically insignificant. Carlton states that the failure of taxes to show up as an important influence on location is consistent with Schmenner's previous findings.

According to Newman & Sullivan, Carlton's papers are a noteworthy development in location studies. Using firm births and branch plants as the focus of the model is an improvement because they "represent direct observations of capital which is mobile per se, thus avoiding the capital mobility issue."[16] They also laud Carlton's underlying theoretical model which bases his estimating equation on a profit maximizing function.

Newman & Sullivan also point out some of the weaknesses in this study which helped set the direction of later research. Carlton's study is an interstate sample, but he pools the state corporate and state personal income taxes into one regressor due to potential multicollinearity. Newman & Sullivan disagree with this approach since these taxes could have different effects on a location decision.[17] They also consider the size of his sample to be too small and narrow for any generalizations.[18] Finally, they question Carlton's conditional logit techniques which Bartik later addresses and modifies in his 1985 study. On balance, however, Carlton's work marks the beginning of location models with estimating equations based on profit maximization functions using births or employment as the regressands.

INTERSTATE AND INTERMETROPOLITAN STUDIES SINCE 1979

The work up to and including Carlton's studies predominantly concluded that taxes are not a critical factor in location decisions. The multitude of studies published after Carlton's have yielded mixed results. Not only are there a vast array of dependent variables examined, but the focus of the conclusions are as diversified as the sample regions and time periods covered.

Most studies of tax differential effects are on an interstate basis using data aggregated to the state level or encompass a large number of Metropolitan Standard Areas (MSAs) to analyze intermetropolitan tax differentials. In either case, these studies typically use cross section data with a dependent variable that is some measure of industrialization or economic growth. The explanatory variables span an array of several different taxes, such as state income taxes (personal and corporate), property taxes and capital taxes.

Hodge's (1979) study analyzes regional investment in 42 MSAs for the period 1963-1975 for four different industries. The corporate tax variable is negative and statistically significant for only the furniture industry. Property taxes have a statistically significant negative affect on investment in the furniture and apparel industries. Both tax variables are not statistically significant for the other two industries (electronics; rubber and plastics).

Romans & Subrahmanyam (1979) investigate taxes versus fiscal benefits in terms of firm location decisions. The dependent variables in their single equation OLS regression models are the rate of growth in each of the following: state personal income; per capita income; or nonagricultural employment for the 48 continental states. They conclude that if taxes are used for transfer payments (and not public goods) firms locate elsewhere. The tax variables in their analysis include proxies for tax levels and tax progressivity. Tax levels are measured by state tax effort of personal taxes and state tax effort of business taxes, both as calculated by the ACIR.[19] The average marginal state personal tax rate with respect to family income is used as a measure of tax progression. Higher marginal personal tax rates have a negative effect on employment. However, the coefficient for state tax effort for the level of business taxes is positive and statistically significant, indicating that states with higher tax rates on business were growing faster, either because businesses were getting something in return for the taxes they paid, or else locational rents were high enough to allow higher tax rates on business without discouraging industry location or growth.[20]

In contrast, Benson & Johnson (1986) use a slightly different dependent variable than Romans & Subrahmanyam. Their dependent variable is a state's per capita capital expenditure for new plant and equipment divided by the same average measure derived across 48 states. Using a pooled time series for 1966 to 1978, they find the state tax variable to be negative and statistically significant with a two year lag.

Other interstate studies, such as Church (1984), Helms (1985), Wasylenko & McGuire (1985), and Mofidi & Stone (1990), find that taxes do not deter investment if there are fiscal benefits offsetting them. Out of these four publications, Helms (1975) stands out as the most instrumental in advancing this evidence. His pooled cross section time series study of state personal income growth for 1965-1979 was the first to use a government budget constraint in the model. The tax variables have the expected negative signs and are statistically significant. The coefficients for the expenditure variables are positive for those which benefit workers and firms, such as education, highways, and public health and safety. However, the coefficient for transfer payments is negative. His conclusion is that state and local taxes retard economic growth when the revenue is used for transfer payments, but not when it is used for public services. He states that "the favorable impact on location and production decisions provided by the enhanced services may more than counterbalance the disincentive effects of the associated taxes."[21]

Papke & Papke (1986) is often cited as an interstate study supporting the hypothesis that taxes are a strong determinant of capital investment per worker. Their tax variable called AFTAX is an aggregation of sales, property and corporate income taxes of the state into a measure of an after-tax rate of return. They find tax burdens to be statistically significant. Specifically, industries in states with higher after-tax rates of return (lower tax levels) attract more capital investment per worker. Later publications by Papke in 1987[22] and 1989[23] both corroborate these findings using different industries and time periods. However, a later study by Papke (1991) for 22 states over a 20-year period for five different industries had mixed results. The furniture industry and the electronic components industry both had "highly elastic responses to the level of effective tax rates" (-0.081 and -0.059 respectively),[24] whereas the book publishing industry had a small negative elasticity and the apparel and communication equipment industries had positive elasticities. Another study by Papke 1991[25] using the same data, but estimating the effect on firm births instead of capital investment expenditures across states, found that "a high state and local marginal effective tax rate reduces the number of firm births for half of the industries examined."[26]

Testa (1989) analyzes the percentage change in employment growth in 75 of the largest MSAs from 1976-1985. His tax variable is the percentage change in per capita state and local taxes. He finds significant negative tax effects on the percent change in manufacturing employment, total employment, and nonmanufacturing employment growth.

Munnell (1990) examines the relationship between state employment growth and public infrastructure in 1970-80 and 1980-88. Her tax variable includes state and local taxes as a percent of state personal income. The tax burden variable is consistently negative and statistically significant across the four models estimated. Her results also indicate that a state's investment in public capital also had a significant positive effect on state employment growth.

Friedman et al (1992) investigate what attracts foreign multinational corporations (MNCs) to locate branch plants in the 48 continental states between 1977 and 1988. Using a conditional logit model, they find that local taxes (as measured by state and local tax receipts divided by state population) are negative and statistically significant for both Japanese and European MNCs.

While many of these studies find significant effects of various measures of business taxes, the dependent variables, time periods, geographic units, and tax variables are so diverse, it is difficult to summarize the results into a definitive conclusion. Moreover, property taxes are not separately specified in the models.

INTERSTATE STUDIES AND PROPERTY TAXES

The interstate studies published since 1979 either do not include a property tax variable, or they use an aggregated or average tax rate for the entire state. In a study by Plaut & Pluta (1983), the coefficient on the property tax variable has the wrong sign. It is positive and statistically significant.[27] They offer an explanation for this surprising result. Based on their principal components analysis, they conclude that high property taxes are indicative of a locally-dominated tax system as opposed to a state-dominated system. They hypothesize that firms are attracted to locally-dominated tax systems because:

> firms are able to avoid high overall state taxes, pick a community with low local taxes, and/or choose a community with the tax/expenditure system that best meets their needs.[28]

Their study includes a comprehensive list of fiscal variables, both taxes and expenditures. In general, however, they conclude that fiscal variables do not have a major impact on manufacturing growth as measured by the percent changes in real manufacturing value-added, in manufacturing employment, or in real manufacturing capital stock. Instead land, labor, energy and climate variables are more important.

A prominent study is Bartik's 1985 conditional logit model using a Cobb-Douglas production function. He investigates the effect of several factors on the state location of 1,607 manufacturing branch plants from 1972 to 1978. Bartik takes care to develop business tax variables to correspond to effective tax rates. In particular, the property tax variable is based on ACIR data on the percentage of business property of a state's assessed property values divided by the ACIRs estimates of each state's total business assets. The results indicate that public infrastructure, proxied by highway miles per square mile, is a strong magnet, while high unionization is a strong repellent of firm location. The corporate income tax is the only tax which negatively influences a location decision. The property tax variable coefficient is negative, but is not statistically significant. This paper is generally cited as evidence that taxes are not a critical factor in location decisions.

Interestingly, in his 1989 publication Bartik uses different data and a slightly different focus. This time he investigates small business start-ups (births) by state instead of branch plants. The periods in question are 1976-78, 1978-80, and 1980-82. Using panel data from the U.S. Establishment and Longitudinal Microdata (USELM) file of the Small Business Data Base,[29] Bartik uses a conditional logit model to estimate the location effect of a lengthy list of market, tax, public service, financial market, and demographic variables, in addition to other variables, such as unionization, land area, environmental regulations, and regional dummies. In this study, the property tax is calculated as an average property tax rate on FHA insured single family houses times the assessment/sales price ratio for commercial/industrial properties, divided by the assessment/sales price ratio of single family properties.[30]

For small business start-ups, the property tax and the corporate tax are the only tax variables which have negative and statistically significant coefficients in both the pooled cross-section and panel regressions. Bartik surmises that the strong negative effect of property taxes may exist because property taxes must be paid regardless of profits. Since many businesses are not profitable in their first few years, high property taxes are much more of a concern than profits-based taxes.[31] In conjunction with the tax results, the public services variables indicate that fire protection services and local school spending have strong positive effects on small business births, while welfare expenditures have negative effects.

Deich's 1989 study is somewhat different because the dependent variable is a state's births of new branch plants divided by the number of national new branch plants from 1967-1982. He concludes that state and local taxes influence the location of branch plants in some manufacturing industries, but the estimated negative tax effect is small. A weakness of his work is that state income tax rates and local property tax rates are combined into one variable. Therefore, his results in regards to the impact of property taxes alone are difficult to pinpoint.

Carroll and Wasylenko (1994) extend their empirical work from 1989 which indicated that state employment growth in the 1980s was not related to fiscal factors. In their 1994 research analyzing state employment growth from 1967-1988, they find evidence of a structural shift between 1976 and 1983. Fiscal variables influenced manufacturing employment growth in the states in the 1970s, but not in the 1980s. In contrast, fiscal variables did not significantly impact employment growth in the nonmanufacturing sector in either decade. They include a property tax variable in their estimations which consists of the state and local property tax revenues per $100 of personal income. Their results indicate that high property tax revenues had a statistically significant negative impact for nonmanufacturing employment in both decades, but only had a statistically significant negative effect for manufacturing employment in the 1967-1983 period, and not in the 1984-1988 time frame.

Duffy (1994) analyzes the percent change in state manufacturing employment growth in 19 two-digit industries in the 48 continental states from 1954-1987. The property tax variable in the model is one of three tax variables. He uses 1960 data as the basis for per capita property taxes. The other tax variables are 1970 per capita state and local general revenues and the 1967 ACIR tax effort index divided by the ACIR tax capacity index. Out of the 19 industries examined, property taxes were statistically significant in only the apparel, petroleum, and miscellaneous manufacturing industries.

Interstate studies are not conclusive in determining the effects of property taxes on the location decisions of firms. Not only are the results mixed across the studies, but they all suffer from a data aggregation problem in terms of the property tax variables they select. The property tax is a tax levied by cities as well as by independent school districts, county governments, and special districts. Generally, the interstate studies use the average effective rates of either one or all the property taxes levied by jurisdictions within a state. Interstate studies, therefore, lack credibility in offering policy makers definitive evidence that property taxes are critical factors in regional economic development.

INTERMETROPOLITAN STUDIES AND PROPERTY TAXES

Intermetropolitan studies use a large number of Metropolitan Standard Areas (MSAs) as their focal point instead of the 48 or 50 states. The number of MSAs varies by researcher as does the scope of the fiscal variables included in the models. Many of these studies do not include a separate variable to test the effects of property tax differentials. For example, Luce (1990) uses the ACIR estimate of local tax effort[32] which "controls for differences in the size of local tax bases and includes income, property, sales and other taxes levied by state, county, municipal and school authorities."[33] His results do not indicate significant tax effects in employment change in manufacturing industries for the 38 MSAs he investigated between 1972-77. However, he finds significant tax effects for the same MSAs during the 1977-82 period for high-tech manufacturing firms, but not for low-tech manufacturing firms. O'hUallachain & Satterthwaite (1992) use Wheaton's (1983) measure of corporate state tax burdens calculated as total corporate taxes divided by net business income. The corporate taxes include property taxes, corporate income taxes, unemployment payroll taxes, license fees, and other charges. Of the 37 industries analyzed, their results indicate statistically significant corporate tax effects in the employment growth of only three industries—banking, amusement and recreation services, and legal services. Eberts (1991) includes a variable simply called "taxes" which is not explicitly defined in the study. He estimates the effect of public capital growth on firm openings from 1976-1978 for 40 MSAs. The coefficient for the tax variable is statistically significant only for small firms (fewer than 100 employees), but not for large firms (greater than 500 employees).

Several intermetropolitan studies include a separate variable for property taxes. Gyourko's 1987 study analyzes the effect of taxes on the factor intensity of manufacturing activity across 30 cities in 1972 and 1977. He finds that high property tax cities have more labor-intensive manufacturing bases. Bradbury & Ladd (1988), on the other hand, analyze the relationship between tax rates and city property tax bases for 86 large US cities in 1972, 1977, and 1982. They conclude that property taxes affect a locale's economy because a 10% increase in a city's property tax decreases its property tax base by about 1.5%.[34]

Crihfield's 1989 study estimates the percentage change in labor demand in manufacturing industries in over 200 MSAs between 1963-1977. The coefficients for variables controlling for the beginning of the period property taxes and for the change in effective county property taxes are negative in all five models, and statistically significant in two of them. His later study published in 1990 uses the same variables in four models to estimate the percentage change in metropolitan manufacturing output for the same time period across

217 MSAs. Once again, the property tax variables are negative in all the models, but are statistically significant in three of them. In both studies, the property tax variables are proxies to "at least partly capture differences in local gross capital costs."[35]

McConnell and Schwab (1990) use a conditional logit model to examine the impact of a variety of county characteristics on the locations of 50 new branch plants in the motor vehicle industry between 1973 and 1982. The geographical scope spans 27 states encompassing 2,500 counties. Although their primary focus is on the impact of environmental regulation on industry location decisions, their study includes a county property tax rate "to capture intra-state differences in taxes."[36] State taxes are measured using the Wheaton tax variable.[37] In the four versions of their model, the county property tax variable is negative but is not statistically significant. State taxes are significant in two of their models—the basic model and one controlling for education expenditures. State taxes are not significant in the models controlling for welfare expenditures and regional dummies.

Tannenwald and Kendrick (1995) extend Papke's work using the AFTAX model[38] to evaluate the business tax climate of 15 cities in 1986 and 1993. Five of the cities were in the state of Massachusetts, the other ten were located in states competing with Massachusetts in the five major industries prevalent in the state. The biggest extension of Papke's work is that Tannenwald and Kendrick attempt to include more comprehensive property tax measures in the AFTAX measure of tax burdens because they do not have to aggregate statewide tax rates as Papke did. They report large tax effects such that "a state can greatly boost capital spending within its borders by lowering marginal tax burdens on business fixed investment."[39]

INTRAMETROPOLITAN STUDIES

Intrametropolitan studies have certain advantages in examining whether or not state and local taxes, and specifically property taxes, actually affect location decisions. Newman & Sullivan point out that labor mobility across communities within a metropolitan area is high, and capital is mobile also. In addition, competition across communities restricts potential tax shifting. Therefore, the demand and cost of resources other than land can be assumed to have little cross variation, allowing the researcher to concentrate on the factors that do vary, namely taxes. More importantly, instead of using tax averages, tax rates are often identifiable. Two disadvantages are that the sample sizes tend to be small, making generalizations shaky, and the modelling of site supply can sometimes be difficult.[40] In addition to Fox's work of the Cincinnati and Cleveland areas described previously, the other noteworthy studies entail regions of either one or more adjacent cities or, in the case, of Howland (1985), counties in a tri-state area. Wasylenko (1980) and Erickson & Wasylenko (1980) both analyze the suburban location decisions of single-digit SIC industries leaving the central city in Milwaukee City from 1964-1974. They find that agglomeration economies and the available labor force are more important than fiscal variables. However, in extended work, Wasylenko (1988) excludes localities which zone out industrial or commercial sites, and finds that the effective property tax is negative and statistically significant for manufacturing and wholesale trade. This is similar to the results of Charney's (1983) five-year study of Detroit at the zip code level. He finds that the property tax rate is a significant negative location factor to relocating firms (not births), and in fact, the significance is more pronounced as the size of the firm increases.

McGuire (1983) analyzes the impact of tax rate differentials on firm location decisions in a metropolitan area, controlling for the degree to which industries pollute the environment and communities zone for "good" polluters and against "bad" ones. For the 119 communities in a seven-county area in Minneapolis-St.Paul from 1975-1980, she finds that property tax rates have a negative and statistically significant impact on the value of all new firms and additions. Her property tax variable is a weighted average of the levies for the community, school district, watershed district, county, and any other taxing authority. The weights are based on the total taxable property values of the portion of the school districts that are contained in the community.[41]

In extended work published in 1987, McGuire uses the same data with a different model. The perspective of the model is in the opposite direction of causation. McGuire investigates how relocating firms and their environmental impact on communities affect property tax rates. The percentage change in property tax rates from 1975-1980 is the dependent variable regressed against the value of taxable property (capital), the pollution content of firms that located in the community during the period, and several control variables. She concludes that property taxes vary inversely with the amount of tax base provided by newly locating firms.

In contrast, Howland (1985) examines whether or not property tax rates and tax abatement programs influence firm births. The scope of her study includes the machine tool and electronic components industries in 106 counties in New Jersey, Maryland, Virginia, and the District of Columbia. Her results indicate that property tax rates and tax abatement programs do not influence births. Instead, wages, the pool of entrepreneurs available, the distance of the labor force, and urbanization economies do.

McHone's (1986) often-cited study concentrates on the Philadelphia MSA for the year 1970. Excluding the center city, he applies Fox's model to data for 95 communities in the four suburban Pennsylvania counties of the Philadelphia MSA because the majority of new industrial location activity is occurring in the suburbs. He notes that in 1963, 29% of MSAs had more manufacturing employment in suburbs than central cities. By 1977 this fraction had grown to 50%.[42] Using a two-stage least squares, cross-sectional approach, McHone determines that "local government fiscal activities have a statistically significant influence on the spatial pattern of industrial activity through both the demand and supply sides of the market for industrial development rights."[43] Newman & Sullivan criticize McHone's work because as a study encompassing the supply-side of the market, he does not include land price in his regressions.[44]

White's 1986 study investigates whether or not local property taxes affect firm location using pre- and post-Proposition 13 California counties. After Proposition 13 was passed, local property taxes were no longer determined by each municipality, but were set at a uniform rate state-wide. Her dataset encompasses thirty of California's fifty counties for 1977 and 1981 for 54 SIC codes. Her results provide support that property taxes have a significant negative effect on the retailing-services sector. A one percent decrease in the property tax causes a 6% increase in firm births, a 6% increase in employment and a 15% increase in payroll.[45] In contrast, her results do not indicate that manufacturing firms are as sensitive to a change in property taxes. The coefficients for the change in property tax variable in all three manufacturing models are not statistically significant.

Gyourko's 1987 analyzes both new firm activity and employment changes in the five counties in the Philadelphia MSA from 1980-1983. His results indicate that high property taxes led to depressed levels of new manufacturing firms in some of the outlying counties. High population densities, business land availability and access to interstate highways encouraged manufacturing firm births. In contrast, he finds that property tax differentials did not have a significant impact on firm births in the services sector, nor did other local economic variables. Population density was the only factor which consistently encouraged firm births of service businesses.

Sander's 1989 study examines the effects of local taxes and schooling on private nonfarm employment growth in Illinois from 1980-1986. The data is on the county level. There is a variable for property taxes, but it aggregates the school and municipal property taxes. Sander finds that "property taxes have a highly significant negative effect on employment growth."[46]

An intrastate, intercounty study by Fox and Murray published in 1990 focuses on firm location and start-ups in the 95 counties in Tennessee for 1980-1986. In addition to business and local sales taxes, they test whether or not equalized property tax rates have a negative impact on business location decisions. In all six of their models, the coefficient of the property tax variable is negative, but it is statistically significant only for firms with fewer than five employees. They conclude that property tax rate differentials do not impact on the location decisions of larger firms.

Woodward (1992) analyzes the locational determinants of Japanese branch plant location decisions in the United States for 1980-89. The paper separates state and county decisions. A separate conditional logit model is used to determine the explanatory variables for a county given that a state has been chosen. The county regression results indicate that per capita property taxes are not statistically significant in all four of the models specified. Instead, manufacturing agglomeration and land area were important determinants for Japanese branch plant location sites. Moreover, areas with low unemployment and poverty rates, and high levels of educated, productive workers were more likely to be selected.

McDonald (1993) examines the effect of local property tax differences on the size of the commercial and industrial property tax base in the six counties across the metropolitan Chicago area for 1982, 1985 and 1988. His work is very similar to Ladd and Bradbury's 1988 research of 86 large cities, except that McDonald concentrates on the commercial and industrial property tax base rather than the total property tax base. Therefore, his work is more indicative of the impact of local property taxes on firm activity. His results indicate that the commercial and industrial tax base is sensitive to changes in the property tax rate. An increase in the property tax rate on commercial and industrial property has a large negative effect on the growth of the commercial and industrial tax base.

Luce (1994) investigates the effects of fiscal variables on the location of jobs and workers in the Philadelphia MSA for 1970 and 1980. The property tax variable is the summation of the effective county, local and school property tax. His results indicate that only services and retail trade employment are significantly impacted by property tax differentials. The manufacturing, wholesale trade, finance and other employment models do not indicate sensitivity to property tax rate differentials.

Peddle (1987) argues that while the theoretical foundations of the intrametropolitan location studies have improved, the empirical techniques used have produced biased and inconsistent estimates. These studies fail to identify the censored and/or truncated nature of the data used. This occurs because not all communities within a MSA have industrial activity or employment. Usually independent variables are observed for all communities in the MSA, not just those with industrial activity. However, in excluding communities which zone out industrial or commercial firms, the data sample distribution is truncated, leading to biasness and inconsistency when using a two-stage least squares estimating technique.

CONCLUSION

Bartik's 1991 book provides the most extensive review of the studies of the effects of state and local taxes on business activity. In a brief 1994 survey article, he reports that 70% (57 studies) of all of the studies he reviewed published between 1979 and 1991 indicated at least one significantly negative tax effect. Seventy-two percent (19 studies) of the studies published from 1991-94 provided evidence of at least one significantly negative tax effect.[47] In his review of just the intrametropolitan location studies and the effects of property taxes, Bartik concludes that there seems to be a "general consensus across studies that property taxes have a large effect on intrametropolitan business location."[48]

In all the studies reviewed in this chapter, the dependent variables chosen by the researchers to measure the level of economic activity are quite diverse. They run the gamut of small business starts, branch plant starts, various employment statistics, per capita income, investment per worker, firm births, and changes in either firm births, income, employment, or taxes. However, the question of whether or not property taxes affect local economic activity is still controversial. The interstate and intermetropolitan studies get mixed results, but the property tax data is aggregated and averaged in many different ways. The intrametropolitan studies lead to less data aggregation, but the regions are rather narrow. In addition, the intrametropolitan studies which omit communities with zoning have the data truncation problem noted by Peddle. In spite of these weaknesses, the findings for these studies are not conclusive either. Some of the intrametropolitan researchers, such as McDonald (1993), Sander (1989), Wasylenko (1988), Charney (1983), McHone (1986), and Fox (1973) conclude that local taxes are an important factor in a region's economy. Other studies, such as those by Wasylenko (1980), Erickson & Wasylenko (1980), McGuire (1983), Howland (1985), and Woodward (1992) determine that nonfiscal factors[49] are more instrumental in stimulating economic development than local tax and expenditure packages. Other intrametropolitan studies, such White's, Gyourko's, or Luce's show that it depends on the sector, but there is not consensus on which sector. White finds property tax differentials depress the services sector, but not the manufacturing sector. Gyourko's results are the opposite. Fox and Woodward determine that high property tax rates deter business start-ups of small firms, but not firms with more than five employees. Luce finds tax sensitivity for only the services and retail trade sectors.

This study has several distinctions to contribute to the literature surveyed. First, since this study is for one state, taken at the county level, it will avoid the data truncation problem noted by Peddle because there is not a single county which completely zones out industrial or commercial activity. Secondly, each property tax faced by a firm will be individually represented as an independent variable to determine its influence on the dependent variable. This, in itself, will be a different approach than all the other studies which average or aggregate municipal, school, and county property taxes together. While the Fox and Murray (1990) study is also an intrastate, intercounty study, they do not isolate the impact of school versus municipal property taxes. Finally, this study will develop an augmented model to investigate whether or not the dispersion or variation of school and municipal property tax rates in a county affects the level of firm location activity in the county.

NOTES

1. Michael Wasylenko, "The Location of Firms: The Role of Taxes and Fiscal Incentives," in *Urban Government Finance: Emerging Trends* edited by Roy Bahl (Beverly Hills: Sage Publications, 1981), 156 & 157.

2. Ibid., 158.

3. Ibid., 159.

4. John F. Due, "Studies of State-Local Tax Influences on Location of Industry," *National Tax Journal* (June 1961): 171.

5. Ibid.

6. ACIR is an acronym for Advisory Commission on Intergovernmental Relations.

7. Barry M. Moriarty, ed., *Industrial Location and Community Development*, (Chapel Hill: Univ. of N.C. Press, 1980), 252.

8. William H. Oakland, "Local Taxes and Intraurban Industrial Location: A Survey," in *Metropolitan Financing and Growth Management Policies* edited by G.F. Break (Madison: Univ. of Wisconsin Press, 1978), 20.

9. Ibid., 22.

10. William A. Fischel, "Fiscal and Environmental Considerations in the Location of Firms in Suburban Communities," in *Fiscal Zoning and Land-Use Controls* ed. by E.S. Mills and W.E. Oates, (Mass: Lexington Books, 1975), 155.

11. Ibid., 156.

12. Wasylenko, 182.

13. 39 MSAs for Fabricated Plastic Products, 24 for Communication Transmitting Equipment, and 26 for Electronic Components.

14. Dennis W. Carlton, "The Location and Employment Choices of New Firms: An Econometric Model with Discrete and Continuous Endogenous Variables," *The Review of Economics and Statistics* (August 1983): 444.

15. Ibid.

16. Robert J. Newman and Dennis H. Sullivan, "Econometric Analysis of Business Tax Impacts on Industrial Location: What Do We Know, and How Do We Know It?" *Journal of Urban Economics* 23 (March 1988): 225.

17. Ibid., 226.

18. Only 24-39 MSAs are included, depending on the industry.

19. State and local tax effort is a concept developed by the Advisory Commission on Intergovernmental Relations in its publication entitled *Measuring the Fiscal Capacity and Effort of State and Local Areas*, Washington D.C., 1972. Tax effort is measured by state and local taxes as a percentage of revenue capacity (or potential yield). Actual state and local tax revenues are divided by the state tax revenues which would have been received if all of a state's tax rates were equal to the national average.

20. Thomas Romans & Ganti Subrahmanyam, "State and Local Taxes, Transfers and Regional Economic Growth," *Southern Economic Journal* 46 (1979): 439.

21. L.Jay Helms, "The Effect of State and Local Taxes on Economic Growth: A Time Series-Cross Section Approach," *Review of Economics and Statistics* (Nov. 1985): 574.

22.   Leslie E. Papke, "Subnational Taxation and Capital Mobility: Estimate of Tax-Price Elasticities," *National Tax Journal* 40, no. 2 (1987): 191-203.

23.   Leslie E. Papke, "Taxes and Other Determinants of Gross State Product in Manufacturing: A First Look," *Proceedings of the 82nd Annual Conference* held by the National Tax Association-Tax Institute of America (1989): 274-282.

24.   Leslie E. Papke, "The Responsiveness of Industrial Activity to Interstate Tax Differentials: A Comparison of Elasticities," in *Industry Location and Public Policy* edited by Henry W. Herzog, Jr. and Alan M. Schlottmann (Knoxville: Univ. of Tennessee Press, 1991), 128.

25.   Leslie E. Papke, "Interstate Business Tax Differentials and New Firm Location," *Journal of Public Economics* 45 (June 1991): 47-68.

26.   Ibid., 49.

27.   Schmenner, Huber & Cook (1987) obtain the same result.

28.   Thomas R. Plaut & Joseph E. Pluta, "Business Climate, Taxes and Expenditures, and State Industrial Growth in the United States," *Southern Economic Journal* (July 1983): 114.

29.   This is the same source of data used in this study.

30.   Timothy J. Bartik, "Small Business Start-Ups in the United States: Estimates of the Effects of Characteristics of States," *Southern Economic Journal* 55, no. 4 (April 1989): 1009.

31.   Ibid., 1014.

32.   See endnote 19 for an explanation of the calculation.

33.   Thomas F. Luce Jr., "The Determinants of Metropolitan Area Growth Disparities in High-Technology and Low-Technology Industries," Working Paper, Department of Public Administration, Pennsylvania State University, 1990, p. 11.

34.   Helen F. Ladd & Katharine L. Bradbury, "City Taxes & Property Tax Bases," *National Tax Journal* 41, no. 4 (Dec. 1988): 503.

35.   John B. Crihfield, "A Structural Empirical Analysis of Metropolitan Labor Demand," *Journal of Regional Science* 29, no. 3 (August 1989): 353.

36.   Virginia D. McConnell and Robert M. Schwab, "The Impact of Environmental Regulation of Industry Location Decisions: The Motor Vehicle Industry," *Land Economics* 66, no. 1 (February 1990): 74.

37.   Wheaton's (1983) measure of corporate state tax burdens is calculated as total corporate taxes divided by net business income. The corporate taxes include property taxes, corporate income taxes, unemployment payroll taxes, license fees, and other charges.

38.   Refer to page 22.

39.   Robert Tannenwald and Christine Kendrick, "Taxes and Capital Spending: Some New Evidence," *Proceedings of the 87th Annual Conference on Taxation 1994* held by the National Tax Association-Tax Institute of America (1995): 118.

40.   Newman & Sullivan, 221 & 222.

41.   Therese J. McGuire, "Essays on Firm Location in a Metropolitan Area" (Ph.D. diss., Princeton Univ., 1983), 78.

42.   W. Warren McHone, "Supply-Side Considerations in the Location of Industry in Suburban Communities: Empirical Evidence form the Philadelphia SMSA," *Land Economics* 62, no. 1 (Feb. 1986): 64.

43. Ibid., 72.

44. Newman & Sullivan, 163.

45. Michelle J. White, "Property Taxes and Firm Location: Evidence from Proposition 13," in *Studies in State and Local Public Finance* edited by Harvey S. Rosen (Chicago: University of Chicago Press, 1986), 104.

46. William Sander, "Local Taxes, Schooling, and Jobs in Illinois," Working Paper No. 75. Office of Real Estate Research, College of Commerce and Business Administration, Univ. of Illinois at Urbana-Champaign, December 1989, p. 3.

47. Timothy J. Bartik, "Taxes and Local Economic Development: What do We Know and What Can We Know?" *Proceedings of the Annual Conference of the NTA-TIA 1994*, (1995): 104.

48. Timothy J. Bartik, "The Effects of Property Taxes and Other Local Public Policies on the Intrametropolitan Pattern of Business Location" in *Industry Location and Public Policy* edited by Henry W. Herzog, Jr. and Alan M. Schlottmann (Knoxville: Univ. of Tennessee Press, 1991), 78.

49. Examples are factors such as wage rates, size of the entrepreneurial pool, and agglomeration economies.

III

Description of the Model

THE NULL HYPOTHESIS

The hypothesis is that local property taxes influence the location decisions of "footloose" firms—that is—those which are not required to locate near their market or their resource base. For example, national manufacturing firms are generally more footloose than service or nonmanufacturing firms which typically require close proximity to their markets. Throughout this study nonmanufacturing firms will consist of the following eight industries: agriculture; mining; construction; transportation and communication; wholesale; retail; finance and insurance; and services.

Formally stated, the null hypothesis examined in this study is: Property tax rate differentials do not affect the location of nascent firms. The following model will be used to test whether or not the null hypothesis can be rejected.

GENERAL MODEL OF FIRM LOCATION

This study will adopt a modified version of the theoretical model of intrametropolitan location of firms presented by Erickson and Wasylenko (1980). Their paradigm is based on the assumption that while firms search a metropolitan area for an optimum location, firms in different industries do not necessarily choose locations based on the same criteria. An optimum location for a firm depends on whether the firm's locational objective is to maximize profits or to minimize costs.

The degree to which a location impacts costs or sales revenue varies by industry. For example, the location of most manufacturing firms does not severely affect sales. These firms can base their location decisions upon a cost minimization objective without much regard for the influence a location has on sales. However, firms in retail and service industries are presumably more closely tied to their markets on a local level. Consequently, their decision not only encompasses cost factors, but must also include sales revenue potential by location. Hence, their site choice is based on a profit maximization objective. Erickson and Wasylenko's paper delineates two different models of firm location. The cost minimization model is directed at manufacturing firms while the profit maximization model is aimed at the retail and service industries.

The cost minimization model starts with a production function of a firm which uses land (L), labor (N), capital (K), and a certain amount of public services (G). In addition, agglomeration economies, or rather, a concentration of firms (CONC) may also impact a firm's output. The production function is:

$$Q = f(L, N, K, G, CONC) \tag{1}$$

The costs of inputs are:
$$C = P_L L + P_N N + P_K (1 + t/r) K \tag{2}$$

where P_L = price of land

P_N = wage rate

P_K = price of capital

t = effective tax rate on K^1

r = discount rate

The firm minimizes costs subject to the constraint of the production function as:

$$\text{Min } C = P_L L + P_N N + P_K (1 + t/r) K - \delta[Q - f(L, N, K, G, CONC)] \tag{3}$$

According to Erickson and Wasylenko, this equation yields a demand for the factors of production as long as second order conditions are satisfied. They specifically note that the demand for land in a municipality is:

$$D_L = f(Q_0, P_N, t, P_L, CONC, G) \qquad (4)$$

In other words, the firm's demand for land is related to output, wages, tax rates, price of land, agglomeration economies and public services. The price of capital is not included because Erickson and Wasylenko assume: 1) the supply of land sites is perfectly elastic; 2) "property taxes are capitalized into the price of land; and 3) most of the burden of the property tax is on capital."[2] Furthermore, they argue that:

> The net price of capital P_K is the same in each municipality while the gross price of capital differs among municipalities by differences between the municipality's property tax rate and the national average property tax rate.[3]

They base their assumptions on the "new view" of incidence of the property tax. The old view is that the burden of industrial and commercial property taxes on improvements gets shifted to consumers while the burden of the tax on residential rental property is shifted to renters. However, Peter Mieszkowski's classic 1972 article on the incidence of the property tax presents a new view. He concludes that "the system of property taxes imposed by local governments decreases the overall return to capital by the average rate of tax in the nation as a whole and changes the supply price of capital to different cities."[4]

Erickson and Wasylenko's second model—the profit maximization model—is devised for the firm whose location may affect its sales as well as its costs because its output is produced primarily for a local market. The firm's objective is:

$$Max \ \pi = P \cdot Q(Z) - C(Q, P_N, t, P_L, G) \qquad (5)$$

where Z is a vector of characteristics which affect market demand, such as population density and per capita income. Since Z varies by location, so does the amount of output.

The demand for land in this case is:

$$D_L = f(P_L, P_N, t, G, CONC, DEN, PCY) \qquad (6)$$

where DEN is population density and PCY is per capita income.

THE AUGMENTED MODEL

According to Erickson and Wasylenko, the demand for land forms the basis of the empirical models.[5] Since a firm birth occurs with a location decision, a formal or informal search for work space inevitably results in a demand for land. Therefore, the equations for the demand for land can be restated as follows:

$$BMAN_C \quad = \quad f(P_L, P_N, t, G, CONC) \tag{7}$$

$$BNOMAN_C \quad = \quad f(P_L, P_N, t, G, CONC, DEN, PCY) \tag{8}$$

where $BMAN_C$ = the number of manufacturing firm births in a county

$BNOMAN_C$ = the number of nonmanufacturing firm births in a county

P_L = price of land

P_N = wage rate

t = effective tax rate on K[6]

G = public services

$CONC$ = agglomeration economies or concentration of firms

DEN = population density

PCY = per capita income.

Equations (7) and (8) will be the starting point for the development of the estimating equations used in this study. The variables of principal interest (the fiscal variables) will be explained first, followed by the control variables.

Effective Tax Rates

Since this is an intrastate study, new firms all face the same federal and state corporate income taxes and sales taxes. There are no local sales taxes. Other local taxes (such as earned income taxes, commuting taxes, and occupational taxes) are on individuals, not on firms. Therefore, the effective tax rate variable (t) will only consist of the total average effective property tax rates in a county. Due to the fact that several layers of local governments levy the property tax, the total average effective property tax rate is:

$$T_A = SCHOOLA + MUNA + CTY \tag{9}$$

where T_A = total average effective property tax rate

SCHOOLA = average effective school property tax rate

MUNA = average effective municipal property tax rate

CTY = effective county property tax rate.

The average property tax rates for school districts and municipalities may not be the best indication of how relative tax rates affect whether or not firms choose a particular site in a county. There may be a wide distribution of property tax rates across the school districts and municipalities in a particular county. The average tax rate may not reveal the extent to which there are low-tax versus high-tax jurisdictions in the county. Firms may locate in a county with a high relative average tax rate because they find low-tax jurisdictions within it. Therefore, the range of property tax rates among a county's school districts and municipalities could be a relevant location decision element.

For example, assume there are two counties, County A, which has only two school districts, and County B which has three school districts. Also assume the distribution of property values are equally divided among the school districts in two counties. In County A, one school district has an effective property tax rate equal to 5 mills, the other is equal to 35 mills. In County B, the three school districts levy property tax rates equal to 5, 10, and 45 mills respectively. In both counties, the average effective property tax rate is 20 mills and the lowest effective school tax rate is the same—it is 5 mills. However the difference between the highest and lowest possible tax rates in County A is 35-5 or 30 mills, while the range in County B is 40 mills (45-5). Assuming all other factors are the same, the optimal jurisdiction for a firm to choose may be the poorest school district in County B because County B offers a larger set of choices of school districts for the firm's employees to reside in.

This example shows that the range of tax rates can also affect the location decision. While the average effective tax rate is the expected value, or the most likely tax rate a firm would face in a county, it does not capture the full array of tax rates a firm could have to pay. Therefore, variables controlling for the spread of the tax rates of the property taxes will be included as follows:

$$t = f(T_A, \text{SCHOODIF}, \text{MUNDIFF}) \qquad (10)$$

Where t = effective tax rate on K from equations (7) & (8)

T_A = Total average effective property tax rates from equation (9)

SCHOODIF = the difference between the highest effective school property tax rate in a county and the lowest

MUNDIFF = the difference between the highest effective municipal property tax rate in a county and the lowest.

The signs are expected to be negative for the average effective tax rates and positive for the ranges or variables controlling for the differences between the high and low tax rate values. The rationale is that as the range increases within a county, this would give a greater range of location choices to both firms and their employees.

Public Services

In the example above, the two counties were assumed to have an equal distribution of property values. This is not true in the real world. It is possible that a particular community could have a low tax rate because it contains sites with high property values. For example, suppose a small suburb has a small number of residents, but a large number of firms which leads to a high level of property values for the size of the community. Even though the tax rates are low, property tax revenues may not be any larger or smaller than other communities in the county. Therefore, in order to determine whether or not this is an attractive locale for a new firm, it is important to consider the public benefits provided by municipalities.

Public goods or services provided by local governments are of interest to firms because they may be services that are either valued or discounted. Three different types of public services are used to control for the level of benefits associated with the various property tax rates paid by firms.

First, the number of instruction dollars spent per student is included in the augmented model to control for the quality of public education provided by the school districts within a county. Testa (1989) uses educational spending per pupil rather than Wasylenko's education spending as a percent of state of income because spending per pupil is more closely related to service output.[7] Luce (1994) also uses school spending per pupil, rather than per capita expenditures. In this study, both an average instruction dollar spent per student amount and the spread between the highest and lowest amounts spent per pupil will be used. The assumption is that higher average instruction dollars spent per student in a jurisdiction indicates a higher quality of education offered.

The expected signs are difficult to predict a priori. Firms may seek low tax jurisdictions in which to locate their plant and equipment, but their employees may want to reside in school districts with good reputations for quality education. Therefore, it is conceivable that firms may also choose a location in close proximity to school districts with high instruction dollars spent per pupil. Counties which possess both low tax jurisdictions and school districts with high instruction dollars spent per pupil may enjoy high firm birth rates. However, counties with low instruction dollars per student could be attractive because they reflect lower school real estate taxes.

Quan and Beck (1987) found that in the U.S. Northeast, expenditures on education had a positive effect on employment.[8] Testa (1989) also finds education spending to be a positive influence on employment growth. Therefore, the sign for the coefficient for the average instruction dollars per student is expected to be positive, but the sign of the difference variable (INSTDIFF) could be positive if firms want a menu of school district qualities, or negative if they want homogeneous spending per pupil across all the school districts, with poorer school districts obtaining more federal and state funding.

It is possible that high municipal property taxes are not a deterrent to firm births if the public services provided by them are highly valued by firms. Therefore control variables for public service expenditures are included in the model. Papke's 1987 study uses per capita fire and police expenditures to signify a public good benefit. Papke's rationale is:

> A significant coefficient on a business service variable would indicate that taxes net-of-services are the relevant consideration supporting the fee for location-specific service notion of taxes. If, on the other hand, the service variable has little or no influence on the level of capital expenditure, tax burdens may be interpreted as a pure cost of location. [9]

Her results indicate a positive relationship between per capita police and fire protection and new capital expenditures. Jones (1990) also finds a positive relationship between police and fire expenditures and economic growth. [10]

Per capita sanitation services are also used in studies to control for the services provided by property taxes. Per capita sanitation services are likely to have a positive correlation to firm births if they are viewed as a public good benefit.

The public services component of the augmented model is defined as G in the following manner:

$$G = f(\text{INSTAVER, INSTDIFF, POLFIR, SANIT}) \quad (11)$$

Where INSTAVER = Average instruction dollars per student spent in a county

INSTDIFF = The difference between the highest and lowest instruction dollars spent per student in a county

POLFIR = Per capita police and fire expenditures in a county

SANIT = Per capita sanitation and sewage expenditures in a county.

Other Variables - Two-Tiered Tax System

In addition to the variables listed in equations (7) and (8), three other factors will be included in the augmented version of the model. First, a variable called D2RATES will control for the fact that there are fifteen different cities located in twelve counties which have a two-tiered property tax system. Under this system, buildings are taxed at a lower rate than land values. According to Rybeck, a two-tier property tax rate system is generally opposed by land speculators and slum landlords, but can generate more municipal property tax revenues while eliciting positive growth rates for businesses.[11]

The fact that there are four cities in Allegheny County with this property tax system means that a firm with the intentions of choosing a site with a two-tiered property tax system has four different cities to choose from in Allegheny County, versus having only one city to choose from in the eleven remaining counties with two-tiered systems. Therefore, using a dummy variable is not appropriate since Allegheny County would have the same value as all the remaining counties with this property tax system. Therefore, the variable will equal the percentage of land area in a county covered by cities having a two-tiered property tax system.

The rationale for using land area is based on Bartik's dartboard theory.[12] The probability of locating a firm in a county depends not only on the average characteristics of a county, but also its land area. Land area is used as a proxy for the number of potential sites. If a dart is thrown randomly on a map of two counties identical in all aspects except size, then the county with twice as many sites should have twice the probability of having the dart land on it, and therefore be chosen for the location of a new firm.

The fifteen cities with a two-tiered property tax system are located in twelve different counties. These counties will have a value greater than zero, but less than 100.[13] The expected sign of the coefficient is hard to predict a priori. Land intensive firms will be deterred by this property tax system. Presumably manufacturing firms will be more land intensive. Therefore, a negative coefficient is expected. However, a positive coefficient is plausible for nonmanufacturing firms because they tend to be less land-intensive. This result could lend credence to the higher growth rates found by Rybeck.

Other Variables - Credit and R&D

A second variable to be added to the augmented model is a factor to account for industrial development activity in a county. The availability of credit lines, either from banks or industrial development bonds, are generally believed to be positively correlated to the number of new or expanding firms in a region.

Thirdly, according to Malecki, manufacturing sites frequently also require some product-oriented research and development as new products are developed and enter production.[14] R&D projects are often funded by industry and therefore, relative proximity to research and development laboratories can be an attractive factor in a location decision. A positive relationship is expected between a variable for R&D facilities and firm births.

The Entire Model and the Control Variables

A restatement for the augmented model, substituting equations (10) and (11) into equations (7) and (8), and adding the three additional variables noted above, is as follows:

$$
\text{BMAN}_C = f(P_L, P_N, \text{SCHOOLA, MUNA, CTY, SCHOODIF,} \\
\text{MUNDIFF, INSTAVER, INSTDIFF, POLFIR,} \\
\text{SANIT, D2RATES, CREDIT, R\&D, CONC}) \quad (12)
$$

$$
\text{BNOMAN}_C = f(P_L, P_N, \text{SCHOOLA, MUNA, CTY, SCHOODIF,} \\
\text{MUNDIFF, INSTAVER, INSTDIFF, POLFIR,} \\
\text{SANIT, D2RATES, CREDIT, R\&D, CONC, DEN,} \\
\text{PCY}) \quad (13)
$$

The control variables will entail measures of agglomeration economies, land prices, average wages, and a dummy variable to designate whether or not a county is in a Metropolitan Standard Area (MSA). In general, the signs of the agglomeration variables and the dummy variable are expected to be positive. That is, firms tend to gravitate to metropolitan centers. They can often lower their transportation and production costs in areas with a high concentration of other firms.

General theory regarding a firm's demand for the factors of production leads to the expectation that the coefficients of the prices of land and labor will be negative. However, positive coefficients are possible if firms seek labor that is more productive or skilled and land that is closer to metropolitan areas with higher rent gradients. For example, several studies, such as Deich's[15] and also Howland's,[16] result in a positive coefficient for land price. Perhaps this result is due to agglomeration effects or, as Howland reasons, high land values may attract firms because of "an association between a high assessable tax base and high quality schools and services."[17]

Nonmanufacturing firms tend to locate close to their markets. The variables to control for potential market demand are county per capita income and population density. The coefficients of these variables are expected to be positive. Assuming normal goods predominate in the market place, as per capita income rises, market demand for the goods and services produced by nonmanufacturing firms would increase, leading to more nonmanufacturing firm births. Likewise, a large number of potential consumers in a county is a determinant of greater market demand, leading to more nonmanufacturing births to fulfill it.

CONCLUSION

The parameters of the variables in equations (12) and (13) of the entire augmented model will be estimated using the method of ordinary least squares (OLS). The next chapter describes the particular data used as measures for the theoretical variables outlined in the model above. Chapter five will report and interpret four sets of regression estimates. First, manufacturing firm births will be regressed using only the average fiscal variables, omitting the ranges. This regression will be a benchmark to obtain parameters as they are generally estimated by researchers. Then the model will be re-estimated, this time including the ranges of the fiscal variables, as well as the average variables. Both sets of results will be compared to determine if the augmented model yields different results. The same technique will be followed for estimating nonmanufacturing firm births.

NOTES

1. Erickson and Wasylenko do not specify particular taxes on this variable, such as corporate income and/or real estate taxes.

2. Rodney A. Erickson and Michael Wasylenko, "Firm Relocation and Site Selection in Suburban Municipalities," *Journal of Urban Economics* 8 (1980): 72.

3. Ibid.

4. Peter Mieszkowski, "The Property Tax: An Excise Tax or a Profits Tax?" *Journal of Public Economics* 1 (1972): 74.

5. Erickson and Wasylenko, 73.

6. Erickson and Wasylenko do not specify particular taxes on this variable, such as corporate income and/or real estate taxes.

7. William A. Testa, "Metro Area Growth from 1976 to 1985: Theory and Evidence," Working Paper. Federal Reserve Bank of Chicago, January 1989, p. 19.

8. N.T. Quan and J.H. Beck, "Public Education Expenditures and State Economic Growth: Northeast and Sunbelt Regions," *Southern Economic Journal* 54, no. 1 (July 1987): 369.

9. Leslie E. Papke, "Subnational Taxation and Capital Mobility: Estimates of Tax-Price Elasticities," *National Tax Journal* 49, no. 2 (1987): 195.

10. Bryan D. Jones, "Public Policies and Economic Growth in the American States," *Journal of Politics* 52, no. 1 (February 1990): 230.

11. Walter Rybeck, "Pennsylvania Experiments in Property Tax Modernization," *NTA Forum* (Spr. 1991): 3.

12.   Timothy J. Bartik, "Business Location Decisions in the United States: Estimates of the Effects of Unionization, Taxes, and Other Characteristics of States." *Journal of Business & Economic Statistics* 3, no. 1 (January, 1985): 16.

13.   The only county which has land area equal to city land area is Philadelphia County, but Philadelphia does not have a two-tiered property tax system.

14.   Edward J. Malecki, "Recent Trends in Location of Industrial Research & Development: Regional Development Implications for the United States," in *Industrial Location and Regional Systems* edited by John Rees, et al (NY: J.F. Bergin Pub. Inc., 1981), 223.

15.   Michael Deich, "State Taxes and Manufacturing Plant Location," *NTA-TIA Proceedings of the 82nd Annual Conference* (1989): 293.

16.   Marie Howland, "Property Taxes and the Birth and Intraregional Location of New firms," *Journal of Planning, Education and Research* 4 (1985): 151.

17.   Ibid.

IV

Explanation of Variables

DEPENDENT VARIABLES

The dependent variable is the number of firm births which occurred in each of the 67 counties in the state of Pennsylvania during 1976 to 1980.[1] A firm birth is recorded for any establishment in existence in a county at the end of the time period which did not exist at the beginning of the period. The data is from USELM 76/84 Longitudinal Weighted Data prepared by Social & Scientific Systems, Inc. under contract for the Office of Advocacy of the US Small Business Administration in Washington, D.C.

Regressions will be executed with the following two dependent variables:

BMANU76   -   the total number of births of manufacturing firms which occurred between 1976 and 1980.

BNOMAN76   -   the total number of nonmanufacturing firm births which occurred between 1976 and 1980.

The total number of all firm births in the period is equal to the summation of both manufacturing and nonmanufacturing births.

The number of firm births across the 67 counties in Pennsylvania between 1976 to 1980 were:

FIRM BIRTHS	TOTAL	PERCENT
Manufacturing	5,860	8.1
Nonmanufacturing	66,366	91.9
Total New Firms	72,226	100.0

There was at least one birth in each sector in every county. The preponderance of births were in the nonmanufacturing sector, which includes establishments in the following industries: agriculture; mining; construction; transportation and communication; wholesale; retail; finance and insurance; and services. The summary statistics of firm births across PA counties by sector are:

FIRM BIRTHS	MIN	MAX	AVG	STD DEV
Manufacturing	1	676	87	138
Nonmanufacturing	32	9,114	991	1,627
Total New Firms	35	9,717	1,078	1,758

The ten counties with the highest number of firm births between 1976 and 1980 are listed below in descending order.

MANU-FACTURING		NONMANU-FACTURING		TOTAL BIRTHS	
Montgomery	676	Allegheny	9114	Allegheny	9717
Allegheny	602	Philadelphia	7704	Philadelphia	8265
Philadelphia	562	Montgomery	5896	Montgomery	6572
Bucks	414	Bucks	3348	Bucks	3762
Lancaster	341	Delaware	2815	Delaware	3000
York	209	Lancaster	2496	Lancaster	2838
Delaware	185	Lehigh	1973	Lehigh	2123
Luzerne	185	Chester	1936	Chester	2117
Chester	181	Berks	1904	Berks	2084
Berks	180	Luzerne	1828	Luzerne	2014

Eleven different counties appear in the table above. Nine counties appear in each list. The exceptions are York and Lehigh counties. York is in sixth place for manufacturing firm births, while Lehigh county is in seventh place for nonmanufacturing and total firm births. The eleven counties listed are predominately located in the southeastern portion of the state, radiating outward from Philadelphia, the state's only first class city.[2] The exceptions are Luzerne County in the northeast and Allegheny Counties in the southwest. Allegheny

County is the home of Pittsburgh, a second class city. The map on page 58 shows the counties with the highest firm births.

The ten counties with the lowest number of firm births which occurred between 1976 and 1980 are listed below in ascending sequence.

MANU-FACTURING		NONMANU-FACTURING		TOTAL BIRTHS	
Forest	1	Fulton	32	Fulton	35
Fulton	2	Sullivan	35	Sullivan	40
Cameron	4	Forest	44	Forest	45
Sullivan	5	Montour	46	Montour	53
Jefferson	7	Juniata	55	Cameron	59
Montour	7	Cameron	56	Juniata	65
Clarion	10	Potter	82	Potter	97
Juniata	11	Wyoming	109	Wyoming	124
Perry	12	Greene	117	Greene	128
Pike	12	Perry	130	Perry	142

Thirteen different counties appear in the table above. Nine of them are in the northern portion of the state spread out in four clusters (refer to map on page 59). They are predominantly counties with the lowest census counts, ranging from 5,000 people in Forest County to approximately 44,000 in Jefferson County.

SCHOOL PROPERTY TAXES

In 1975, there were 505 school districts in the Commonwealth of Pennsylvania. In fiscal 1975, real estate taxes were $1,187,537,106, which comprised 77.1 percent of the total school taxes collected. Even though taxes increased 7.8 percent over the previous year, the mills on real estate market value decreased 1.3 mills. According to the Pennsylvania Department of Education, the millage decrease was caused by a substantial increase of 13.9 percent in market values.[3] The average mills on market value across the 67 counties amounted

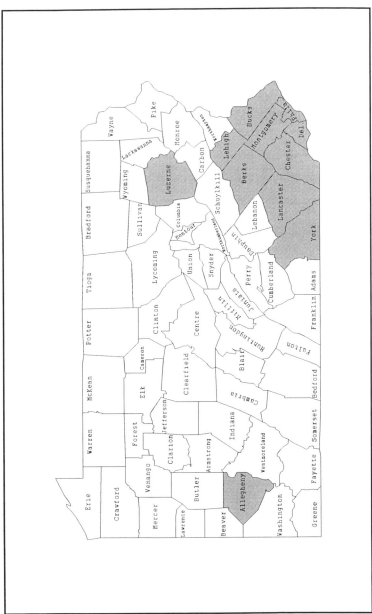

Figure 1: Top Ten Counties with Firm Births From 1976-1980

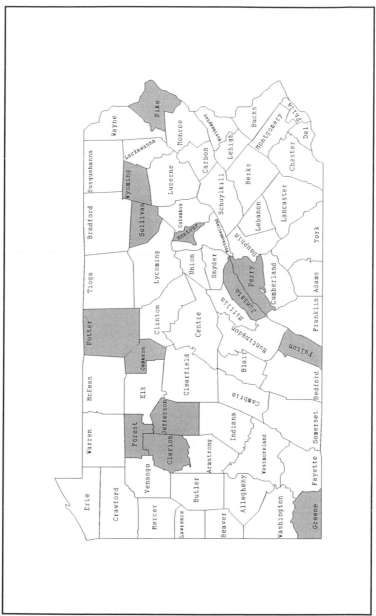

Figure 2: Counties with the Lowest Firm Births From 1976-1980

to 23.8 mills. This was based on total taxes of $1,539,204,750 and a 1974 market value of $64,622,056,500.

Even though assessment is done at the county level, the millage rate varies substantially within a county. In order to compare one county with another, the Pennsylvania Department of Education publishes equalized millage rates and market valuations for each borough, city, and township, by county. The average equalized millage rate for the county's school taxes is a weighted average. Since the Pennsylvania State Tax Equalization Board calculates these equalized millage rates, it is possible to more closely examine the real burden of the tax, thereby avoiding ad hoc calculations and assumptions.

Two different school tax variables will be used to measure, not only the average, but also the range of the high and the low millage rates in a particular county.

SCHOOLAV - School-Tax-Average is stated as the number of mills calculated from total school taxes divided by the total market value of 1974 respectively. Studies generally expect a negative sign to signify a negative relationship between firm births and average school taxes.

SCHOODIF - Measures the difference between the highest equalized millage rate among the school districts in the county and the lowest equalized millage rate. The result is the spread of the mills. For example, the highest equalized millage rate in Adams County is 21.4 mills. The lowest equalized millage rate is 15.8 mills. Therefore, the range or difference is 5.6 mills. The sign of the coefficient is expected to be positive to reflect the range of choices as an attractive factor in a firm's location decision.

The summary statistics for the two school tax variables are:

VARIABLE	DESC	MIN	MAX	AVERAGE	STD DEV
SCHOOLAV	Average	12.4	27.2	21.96	3.25
SCHOODIF	High-Low	0.0	30.0	6.88	4.97

Montgomery County (which is contiguous to Philadelphia County) is unique in that it has a distribution of school districts with the largest difference between the highest and lowest millage rates. The range is from 3.3 to 33.3 mills, resulting in a spread of 30 mills.

There is not another county with a range of millage rates nearly that high. The next highest difference is 15.4 mills in Allegheny County. Ten counties consist of only a single school district, therefore the difference between the highest and lowest millage rates is equal to zero. They are: Cameron, Clinton, Forest, Juniata, Mifflin, Montour, Philadelphia, Pike, Sullivan, and Warren counties. With the exception of Philadelphia County, the remaining nine counties are relatively small in terms of population, ranging from 5,000 to less than 48,000 residents.

Two separate regressions will be executed. The first will use only the average value (SCHOOLAV) as a benchmark for what is generally found in interjurisdictional studies. The average (SCHOOLAV) and range (SCHOODIF) will be used in a second regression to test the hypothesis that firms want to locate in a county with low school taxes, but accessible to better school districts for their employees to reside in.

INSTRUCTION DOLLARS PER STUDENT

This variable is used to control for the quality of public education provided by the school districts within a county. The figures are based on the instruction dollars spent per average daily membership (ADM) for all the school districts operating grades one through twelve. In this study, expenditures on instruction per average daily membership will be used to proxy the educational benefits derived from school real estate property taxes. Total education expenditures consist of those used for instruction, operation and maintenance, administration, transportation, capital outlay and debt, fixed charges and other expenses. Only those used for instruction will be used here, regardless of source of income.

The ADM is used because the Pennsylvania Department of Education considers it to be the most valid measure of per pupil accountability. However, a high instruction cost per pupil does not necessarily imply a high expenditure of local funding since some programs are financed almost entirely by state or federal funds.[4] However, there is a high correlation. This measure is superior to a per capita expenditure. A school district with a large number of school children, other things being equal, will presumably have to spend more per capita to provide the same quality of education than a community with an older age population.

In the fiscal year 1975, statewide expenditures on instruction of $1.7 billion comprised 54% of the total expenditures of the general education fund. In terms of dollars per pupil, the state average was $771.

Since the Pennsylvania Department of Education lists the instruction dollars per student for each school district within a county, the following variables will be used.

INSTAVER - Average-Instruction-Dollars-per-Student is simply the county average across all of the school districts in its jurisdiction. The expected sign of the coefficient is positive to reflect the value firms place on access to quality school systems.

INSTDIFF - This variable is calculated as the difference between the highest amount spent per pupil by a school district in a county and the lowest expenditure per student spent in a county's school district. The sign of the coefficient is difficult to predict a priori. If firms prefer a homogeneous set of quality school districts, then the sign would be negative. If, however, firms prefer an assortment of school districts with varying levels of quality evidenced by a large range of instruction dollars spent per student, then the expected sign is positive.

The ten previously mentioned counties which only consist of a single school district have a range of instruction dollars per student equal to zero. The summary statistics for the average and range of instruction dollars per student are:

VARIABLE	DESC	MIN	MAX	AVE	STD DEV
INSTAVER	Average	504.72	1040.70	686.11	84.80
INSTDIFF	High-Low	0.00	469.11	154.48	115.66

MUNICIPAL AND COUNTY PROPERTY TAXES

Municipal property taxes are local property taxes levied by cities, boroughs and townships. The state average municipal property tax in 1974 was 3.07 mills, approximately 10% of the total average property tax rates faced by a firm. However, the variation of municipal taxes within a particular county is rather large. A firm can locate in a county that has a range of municipal tax rates. For example, some counties have jurisdictions that do not have a property tax at all. In contrast, the highest municipal tax rate was 17.774 mills found in a jurisdiction in Allegheny County. Across the 67 counties in the state there are 2,564 municipalities in the following categories:

MUNICIPALITY	QTY	PERCENT	REMARKS
Boroughs	960	37	
1st class town	91	4	
2nd class town	1,461	57	
1st class city	1		Philadelphia
2nd class city	2		Pittsburgh & Scranton
3rd class city	49	2	
Total	2,564	100	

In addition to municipal property taxes, each county levies a property tax, which is a very small proportion of the total property taxes paid by a firm. For example, the state average of county real estate taxes in 1974 was only 4.58 mills or approximately 15% of the total average property tax mills a firm would face in the Commonwealth. Since every firm in a particular county faces the same county property tax rate, and since the percentages of the municipal and county taxes are a small portion of total real estate taxes, these two tax rates will be added together, and simply referred to as municipal taxes.

Data for both the municipal property tax rates and county tax rates was obtained from the same source. The Commonwealth of Pennsylvania publishes a document entitled *Local Government Financial Statistics*. For each county, the actual tax rate, in mills, is listed for each municipality, as well as the market value of real estate determined by the State Tax Equalization Board (STEB). This provides a uniform measure of taxable real estate valuations rather than assessed valuations, which can range from less than 20% of market value to more than 100%.[5] An assessment ratio is computed from the assessed valuation of real estate versus the market value. For the city of Philadelphia, an assessed valuation of $5.6 billion compared to $10.6 billion of real estate market value results in an assessment ratio of 53.3%. Using the assessment ratio, an "adjusted" mill rate is computed by multiplying the actual mill rate by the assessment ratio. For example, in 1974 the official tax millage rate in the city of Philadelphia is 32.75 mills. However, the adjusted millage rate is much less—17.456 mills—based on a 53.3% assessment ratio of 32.75 actual mills.

The data was obtained for the year 1974 because the effect of property taxes on location decisions is likely to have a lagged effect. For the purposes of using a municipal property tax rate, the adjusted mill rate of each locale in each county will be used as the basis for the following variables.

MUNAVE74 - The average adjusted millage rate of a county computed as an arithmetic mean of the adjusted millage rates of all the cities, boroughs and townships in the county, added to the county property tax millage rate, adjusted as noted above. A negative coefficient is expected, based on the theoretical model built in chapter three.[6] However, given the mixed results of the studies presented in chapter two, the expected sign of this variable is uncertain.[7]

MUNDIF74 - is the range or difference between the highest tax rate in a county versus the lowest rate. A positive coefficient is expected.

The summary statistics are:

VARIABLE	DESC	MIN	MAX	AVERAGE	STD DEV
MUNAVE74	Average	3.79	14.96	7.38	2.31
MUNDIF74	High-Low	0.00	16.76	8.69	3.62

TWO-TIER TAX SYSTEM

A variable called D2RATES will control for the fact that there are fifteen different cities located in twelve counties which have a two-tiered property tax system. As explained in the previous chapter,[8] using a dummy variable is not appropriate because Allegheny County has four cities, whereas the other eleven counties each only have one city with this tax system. A firm with the intentions of choosing a site with a two-tiered property tax system has four different cities to choose from in Allegheny County. In contrast, the firm has only one city to choose from in the eleven remaining counties. A dummy variable would give Allegheny County the same value as the eleven other counties.

Based on Bartik's dartboard theory,[9] the variable will equal the percentage of land area in a county covered by cities having a two-tiered property tax system. The expected sign of the coefficient is hard to predict a priori. Land intensive firms will be deterred by this property tax system. Presumably manufacturing firms will be more land intensive. Therefore, a negative coefficient is expected. However, a positive coefficient is plausible for nonmanufacturing firms because they tend to be less land-intensive.

The total land area for a county was obtained from the *Pennsylvania County Data Book* published for each county by the Pennsylvania Department of Commerce. The land area for the cities was obtained from the 1980 Pennsylvania Census. The value for each county was computed as the ratio of the city square miles to the county square miles multiplied by 100. The nonzero values of the data range from 8.9% in Allegheny County to 0.25% in Clearfield County. The 55 counties that do not have a two-tiered system will have a value equal to zero.

PUBLIC SERVICES

Police and fire expenditures for each county were obtained from the *Local Government Financial Statistics* for the year 1974. They were converted to per capita figures with 1970 population census data. Based on the public benefits argument presented in the previous chapter, a positive coefficient is expected if firms value these services as a public good benefit.

County expenditures for sewers and refuse were obtained from the *Local Government Financial Statistics* for the year 1974. They were converted to per capita figures based upon 1970 census data. A positive coefficient is expected if firms view these services as beneficial public goods rather than costs.

CONTROL VARIABLES

The remaining variables are non-fiscal variables to control for other factors which may influence firm location decisions. A table of summary statistics for these variables is listed at the end of the chapter.

Four variables will be used as proxies for agglomeration effects on the birth of firms. The coefficients are expected to be positive because firms can lower their transportation and production costs in areas with a high concentration of other firms and close access to transportation infrastructure. Their variable names and descriptions are:

IHMILES   -   The number of interstate highway miles in a county.[10]

AIRPORTS   -   The number of airports in a county.[11]

CESTAB76   -   Per capita business establishments in the beginning of the period.[12]

DUMMYMSA -   A dummy variable equal to one if the county is in a metropolitan standard area.[13]

Several researchers have included transportation variables in their models. Coughlin et al (1991), Bartik (1985), Luce (1994) have found highly developed transportation networks to be an attraction for firm location decisions. The Pennsylvania Department of Commerce publishes a *Pennsylvania County Data Book* for each county which lists the number of interstate highway miles and the number of airports in each county in 1975.

CESTAB76 is calculated as the number of business establishments in a county in the beginning of the period divided by the 1970 county population. The number of business establishments is the total number of manufacturing and nonmanufacturing firms in existence in the county in 1976. This is a proxy for the concentration of firms variable used in the Erickson and Wasylenko model.

Per capita loans (CAPITLON) is a crude measure of industrial development activity in a county. The Pennsylvania Industrial Development Authority publishes a summary of the IDB loans issued from 1956. CAPITLON is the number of IDB loans issued in a county from 1956 until 1975 divided by the 1970 population.

Average hourly wages (AVEWAG75) in a county are based on the total payroll figures published in the *Pennsylvania County Business Patterns* for 1975.[14] These are total wages (in nominal dollars) paid to workers in all sectors, excluding government, railroad and self-employed persons. The average was computed from annual payroll data divided by the number of employees in a county, divided by 2000 hours generally worked in a year. The expected sign is difficult to predict a priori. Most studies expect a negative coefficient because firms attempt to minimize costs. However, a positive coefficient is possible if firms are willing to pay a premium for more qualified or skilled labor.

Land prices are included as the variable LANDPR74. *The 1978 Census of Agriculture* publishes the 1974 average cost of a farm acre in each county. Many studies omit this variable because of data limitations. For example, Bartik's 1985 study uses population density as a proxy.[15] Erickson and Wasylenko (1980) use three different proxy variables: the distance of from CBD (Central Business District), dummy variable for access to an interstate highway, and supply of sites.[16] While Howland was able to obtain full market land values for the municipalities in Maryland and Virginia,[17] Deich's 1989 study uses the value of land and buildings per acre for all farms.[18] Papke 1991[19] uses dollar per acre of farm land as well. Due to problems in obtaining good data on land prices for a county, Deich's choice of using farm acre values was selected. As discussed in the previous chapter, the expected sign of the coefficient is difficult to predict a priori. One would expect firms to shun high priced land sites, but firms may be willing to pay higher prices for land if the premium reflects quality public services and schools.

Proximity to research and development facilities can lead to economic development. The Pennsylvania Department of Commerce publishes a *Pennsylvania County Data Book* for each county which lists the R&D facilities and laboratories present in each county. Per capita R&D facilities (CAPRDFAC) will be measured by the number of these establishments in 1976 divided by the 1970 county populations. The year 1976 was the only year the data was available. Two variables will control for market access and potential demand. These variables will be used in the nonmanufacturing regressions. Positive coefficients are expected. They are:

PCY76   -   Per capita income for each county in the year 1976 using 1970 census data.[20]

POPDEN   -   Population density calculated as the number of people in a county divided by the number of square miles.[21]

CONCLUSION

The next chapter will present the regression results for the augmented model developed in chapter three using the variables described above. A table of the summary statistics for all the variables is at the end of this chapter.

The table on the next page is an overview of the independent variables with the corresponding expected sign of the coefficient to be estimated using Ordinary Least Squares (OLS). The primary variables of interest are the fiscal variables. They are the tax rate and public service variables listed as the first nine variables. The control variables are listed following the variable D2RATES.

TABLE 4.1 - THE INDEPENDENT VARIABLES:
DATA SOURCES AND EXPECTED SIGNS

VARIABLE	EXPECTED SIGN	DATA SOURCE	YEAR OF DATA
SCHOOLAV	-	Our Schools Today	1975
SCHOODIF	+		
INSTAVER	+		
INSTDIFF	-		
MUNAVE74	+ or -	Local Govt Financial Statistics	1974
MUNDIF74	+		
POLFIR74	+		
SANIT74	+		
D2RATES	+ or -	Pennsylvania Statistical Abstr.	1980
IHMILES	+	Pennsylvania County Data Book	1975
AIRPORTS	+		
CESTAB76	+	USELM 76/84 Long. Weighted SBA	1976-80
DUMMYMSA	+	Local Govt Financial Statistics	1974
CAPITLON	+	PA Industrial Dev. Authority	1975
AVEWAG75	+ or -	County Business Patterns	1975
LANDPR74	+ or -	1978 Census of Agriculture-PA	1974
CAPRDFAC	+	Pennsylvania County Data Book	1975
PCY76	+	Local Area Personal Income	1976
POPDEN	+	1970 Census	1970

TABLE 4.2 - SUMMARY STATISTICS

VARIABLE	MEAN	MIN	MAXM	STD DEV
BMANU76	87.46	1.00	676.00	137.89
BNOMAN76	990.54	32.00	9114.00	1626.84
SCHOOLAV	21.96	12.40	27.20	3.25
SCHOODIF	6.88	0.00	30.00	5.01
INSTAVER	686.11	504.72	1040.66	84.80
INSTDIFF	154.48	0.00	469.11	115.66
MUNAVE74	7.38	3.79	14.96	2.31
MUNDIF74	8.64	0.00	16.76	3.62
D2RATES	0.33	0.00	8.94	1.30
POLFIR74	15.33	2.05	99.37	13.44
SANIT74	9.71	0.95	33.44	6.87
IHMILES	24.48	0.00	84.77	23.90
AIRPORTS	1.69	0.00	8.00	1.85
PCY76	5590.49	3987.00	8896.00	875.72
CESTAB76	18.34	12.91	36.77	4.29
CAPITLON	1.80E-04	0.00E+00	1.06E-03	1.76E-04
AVEWAG75	4.39	3.24	5.70	0.61
LANDPR74	732.64	301.00	2801.00	482.16
CAPRDFAC	5.92E-05	0.00E+00	9.33E-04	1.27E-04

NOTES

1. Data on firm births was available for two time periods: 1976-1980 and 1980-1984. The earlier time frame was chosen because the macroeconomic environment was expansionary, and therefore, more conducive to new business formation than the latter recessionary time frame.

2. Pennsylvania counties are classified by state law according to population. The 1974 classification is based on the 1970 U.S. Census as follows: Class 1 = more than 1,800,000; Class 2 = 800,000-1,800,000; Class 3 = 500,000-800,000; Class 4 = 225,000-500,000; Class 5 = 95,000-150,000; Class 6 = 45,000-95,000; Class 7 = 20,000-45,000; and Class 8 = less than 20,000. 2.

3. Pennsylvania Department of Education, *Our Schools Today: Public School Financial Statistics Report, 1974-1975*. Vol. 15, no. 7, pp. 21-23, 41.3.

4. *Our Schools Today: 1974-1975*, p. 43.4.

5. Commonwealth of Pennsylvania, *Local Government Financial Statistics: 1974*, May 1976, p. 10.

6. Refer to the last paragraph of page 46.

7. For example, refer to the study by Plaut & Pluta (1983) discussed on page 24.

8. Refer to page 49.

9. Refer to page 49.

10. *Pennsylvania County Data Book* for each county, 1985.

11. Ibid.

12. USELM 76/84 Longitudinal Weighted Data prepared by Social and Scientific Systems, Inc. under contract for the Office of Advocacy of the US Small Business Administration in Washington, D.C.

13. Commonwealth of Pennsylvania, *Local Government Financial Statistics: 1974*, Release No. 1, May 1976.

14. This is the year closest to the beginning of the time period for which data was available.

15. Bartik, (1985): 18.

16. Erickson and Wasylenko, 74.

17. Marie Howland, "Property Taxes and the Birth and Intraregional Location of New firms," *Journal of Planning, Education and Research* 4 (1985): 151.

18. Michael Deich, "State Taxes and Manufacturing Plant Location," *NTA-TIA Proceedings of the 82nd Annual Conference*, (1989): 293.

19. Leslie E. Papke, "The Responsiveness of Industrial Activity to Interstate Tax Differentials: A Comparison of Elasticities," in *Industry Location and Public Policy*, edited by Henry W. Herzog, Jr. and Alan M. Schlottmann (Knoxville: University of Tennessee Press, 1991), 128.

20. Per capita personal income was obtained from *Local Area Personal Income: 1976-1981*, US Department of Commerce, vol. 3, Mideast Region, June 1983.

21. 1970 Census data.

V

Empirical Results

This chapter analyzes the results of four different empirical specifications of the model developed in the previous chapter. The estimates for manufacturing firms are reported first, followed by a discussion of the results for nonmanufacturing firms. For each sector, two different versions of the model are presented. First, a model using only the average values of the tax and expenditure variables is estimated. This version emulates the models generally used by researchers in previous studies. The estimates generated by this "standard" model are compared to the results obtained by the augmented model outlined in chapter three. That is, not only are the average values estimated, but variables for the ranges of the tax rates and instruction dollars per student are included also. The augmented model is expected to have more explanatory power in ascertaining the relationship between property tax rates and the birth of firms. All four regression equations are estimated using the White procedure to correct for heteroscedasticity.[1] Table 5.5 at the end of the chapter presents the results of all four models together.

MANUFACTURING FIRM BIRTHS AND AVERAGE TAX RATES

Births of manufacturing firms which occurred between 1976 and 1980 (BMANU76) were regressed against the average values of the tax and expenditure variables. The variables of primary interest are the fiscal variables shown in the first group in table 5.1. The second group are the control variables.

TABLE 5.1 MANUFACTURING FIRM BIRTHS USING
AVERAGE VALUES
Dependent Variable BMANU76

Variable	Coefficient	T-Statistics	Signif. Level
CONSTANT	-51.83723	-.547044	.5866887
SCHOOLAV	-5.38011	-2.093586	.4119086E-01
INSTAVER	.11047	.812765	.4200585
MUNAVE74	.57566	.187726	.8518220
POLFIR74	3.16322	4.230839	.9471746E-04
SANIT74	-1.83723	-2.261637	.2792836E-01
D2RATES	20.57598	2.923411	.5116367E-02
IHMILES	.36569	1.618606	.1115824
AIRPORTS	23.62756	4.190419	.1082165E-03
CESTAB76	-2.95841	-1.313128	.1949051
DUMMYMSA	5.65931	.311603	.7565885
CAPITLON	24.69652	.896018	.3743724
AVEWAG75	10.54506	.838072	.4058263
LANDPR74	.12526	3.991416	.2069136E-03
CAPRDFAC	26.65140	.871756	.3873490

R^2 = .882 Degrees of Freedom = 52   Adjusted R^2 = .851^2

In regards to the property tax variables, the coefficient for average school tax rates (SCHOOLAV) is negative and statistically significant at a significance level of .04. The estimate for average municipal tax rates (MUNAVE74), however, is not statistically different than zero. Since school property taxes are the largest component of a firm's total real estate tax bill, it is not surprising that average school tax rates would have more explanatory power relative to manufacturing firm births. For example, the state average of school taxes in 1975 was 21.96 mills, thereby comprising 75% of the total millage. By comparison, the state averages for municipal and county property taxes were only 3.07 mills (10%) and 4.38 mills (15%) respectively.

Even though the results indicate that counties with high average school property tax rates have fewer manufacturing firm births, the average instruction dollars spent per student in a county (INSTAVER) does not have a statistically significant effect.

The variable controlling for counties with cities having a two-tier property tax system (D2RATES) has a positive coefficient and is statistically significant at the .005 level of significance. This result agrees with Rybeck's[2] conclusion that a lower tax rate on buildings can invite more economic development. In this case, it has a direct relationship with manufacturing firm births.

While the average municipal tax rate does not seem to be important for manufacturing firm location decisions, municipal public services may be influential elements. The parameter estimates for both police and fire (POLFIR74) and sanitation (SANIT74) expenditures are statistically significant at significance levels of .00009 and .028 respectively. The signs of the coefficients, however, are not the same. Police and fire expenditures have a positive relationship to manufacturing firm births, while sanitation expenditures have a negative relationship.

These variables were included in the model to control for the offsetting benefits of municipal taxes. They were separated into two different categories. Per capita police and fire expenditures were lumped together, but per capita sanitation and sewage were combined into a separate, second variable. Many empirical studies which include control variables for public services do not isolate these expenditures. The results in this study indicate that different public services should not be combined together. The signs are different. Per capita expenditures on police and fire are positively correlated with manufacturing firm births, whereas per capita sanitation expenses are negatively correlated.

The positive coefficient for police and fire expenditures agrees with Papke's[3] findings mentioned in chapter three. It supports her notion that municipal taxes are a fee for location-specific services. Evidently firms value police and fire services.

The negative coefficient for sanitation and sewage services is puzzling. A number of factors may lead to a negative coefficient. High water and sewage expenditures could indicate poor water quality or high congestion. Another aspect to consider is in the state of Pennsylvania, sanitation services are usually financed by water usage fees and not by taxes. The negative sign may indicate that firms consider sanitation and sewage expenditures a cost of location and not a public good benefit. Since police and fire protection services have a high degree of jointness and nonexcludability, they are more likely to be viewed as public goods than are sanitation and sewage expenditures, for which firms pay user fees in addition to municipal property taxes.

Only two control variables are statistically significant. Airports (AIRPORTS) and land prices (LANDPR74) have t-statistics that have levels of significance of less than .0002. A positive coefficient was expected for airports, signaling strong agglomeration effects from this variable. A positive coefficient for land prices has been found by other researchers, such as Deich and Howland,[4] with agglomeration economies generally cited as the rationale. Interstate highway miles (IHMILES) is marginally significant at a level of significance of .11. Once again, the positive coefficient represents agglomeration effects. The remaining control variables have t-statistics that are not statistically different than zero.

The major conclusions drawn from the estimates of the standard model is that high average school tax rates and high sanitation expenditures have a negative effect on manufacturing firm births. A two-tier tax system, police and fire expenditures, and agglomeration economies proxied by the number of airports in a county and high land prices are statistically significant elements in location decisions leading to higher manufacturing firm births. High average municipal property tax rates and the average of instruction dollars spent in a county per student do not seem to matter to manufacturing firm births. Other control variables, such as average wages, per capita loans, per capita research and development facilities, whether or not the county is in an MSA, and a high concentration of firms, do not appear to be important factors in the location decision for a manufacturing firm.

MANUFACTURING FIRM BIRTHS, AVERAGE TAX RATES AND RANGES

The augmented model uses the regression equation reported above, but also includes the ranges of the fiscal variables noted as SCHOODIF, INSTDIFF, and MUNDIF74. These variables measure the ranges between the highest and lowest values for school property tax millage rates, instruction dollars per student, and municipal property tax millage rates respectively. The estimated coefficients and t-statistics are shown in Table 5.2 on the next page.

TABLE 5.2 MANUFACTURING FIRM BIRTHS -
AVERAGES AND RANGES
Dependent Variable BMANU76

Variable	Coefficient	T-Statistics	Signif. Level
CONSTANT	-71.04006	-.756412	.4530239
SCHOOLAV	-6.25115	-2.247402	.2915030E-01
SCHOODIF	6.05094	2.929424	.5142872E-02
INSTAVER	.16603	1.196290	.2373401
INSTDIFF	-.21753	-2.828903	.6749941E-02
MUNAVE74	-1.20087	-3.40654	.7348205
MUNDIF74	-1.78759	-.802593	.4260856
POLFIR74	3.19534	5.529255	.1235926E-05
SANIT74	-13.2862	-1.558356	.1255850
D2RATES	23.65757	3.550509	.8603054E-03
IHMILES	.42593	1.57887	.1207967
AIRPORTS	24.65026	4.899574	.1128970E-04
CESTAB76	-3.53870	-1.656840	.1039423
DUMMYMSA	7.69588	.455983	.6504165
CAPITLON	7.40873	.279400	.7811144
AVEWAG75	18.91951	1.404806	.1663869
LANDPR74	.10874	4.824593	.1408315E-04
CAPRDFAC	19.67793	.534715	.5952651

$R^2 = .907$ Degrees of Freedom = 49   Adjusted $R^2 = .875$

Compared to the standard model, the results for the education variables are similar. The coefficients for average school property tax rates (SCHOOLAV) and instruction dollars (INSTAVER) do not change their signs or statistical significance. That is, average school property taxes have a statistically significant negative relationship with manufacturing firm births at a significance level of .029. Instruction dollars per student are not statistically significant.

Each of the school range variables, however, are statistically significant. The coefficient of the difference between the highest and lowest school property tax rate (SCHOODIF) has a positive sign and is statistically significant at a level of .005. There are more manufacturing firm births as the gap between the highest and lowest school tax rate in a county widens. While firms seem to shun counties with high average school tax rates, they are more likely to locate in counties with larger property tax rate differentials. It seems plausible that they are seeking sites with low school tax rates that are not far from higher tax rate school districts. Assuming higher school tax rates are associated with higher quality school districts, firms may be attracted to the externality of better quality labor pools, or may find employees prefer to reside in higher quality school districts.

INSTDIFF is the difference between the highest and lowest values for the instruction dollars spent per student in a county. The estimate for this parameter is negative and statistically significant at a level of .007. Therefore, counties with wide disparities in the amount of dollars spent per student have less manufacturing firm births. However, the average amount spent (INSTAVER) is not statistically significant.

The findings related to the school tax rate variables (SCHOODIF, SCHOOLAV) seem to contradict those for instruction dollars per student. A possible interpretation is that firms seek out counties with a large disparity in school taxes, but avoid those with a large disparity in instruction dollars per student. Perhaps they are locating in low school tax areas with close proximity to school districts with higher taxes to give their employees options for living in good school districts. These results seem to indicate that firms desire variety in tax levels, but they prefer uniformity in instructional expenditures because lower education expenditures may affect the skill of the labor force. In addition, education expenditures may also be financed by state and federal aid, lowering property tax rates. In any case, empirical studies which only include the average values of these fiscal variables would miss this interesting finding.

As in the estimates for the standard model, a two-tiered tax system and police and fire expenditures are statistically significant, positive factors in manufacturing firm location decisions. As before, the municipal property tax variables are not statistically significant. Evidently, high average municipal property tax rates do not matter, nor the disparity in the ranges of possible municipal tax rates, but good police and fire protection services do. It is plausible that new manufacturing firms are not interested in counties with large differentials in municipal property tax rates. These large differences could signal degraded public service benefits in certain locales.

The estimates for the control variables are very similar to those obtained in the standard model regression. Only airports and land prices are statistically significant at levels of .000011 and .000014 respectively. Once again agglomeration economies are important. However, the concentration of firms in the county (CESTAB76) has a negative relationship to manufacturing firm births at a significance level of .10. It is possible that congestion factors may explain this result.

On balance, the augmented model provides more insight as to how manufacturing firm births are affected by property tax rate differentials. While high average school tax rates are a negative factor in the location decision, the disparity of a county's school tax rates can be a positive element. Evidently firms seek out counties where it is possible to locate in a low tax rate school district, but like having a menu of school district tax rates in which their employees can choose to reside. This is reinforced by the parameter estimates for the instruction dollars per student variables. Evidently good school districts are important, because a county with high average instruction dollars spent per student will tend to have more manufacturing firm births, while firms will tend to shun counties where there is a large disparity in the spending.

The results of the municipal tax rates are also enhanced by the augmented model. Since the average municipal tax rate does not seem to be an important factor in location decisions, it is interesting to note that the range of the municipal tax rates is not a statistically significant element either. New manufacturing firms do not prefer more disparity in municipal tax rates, perhaps because large differentials may indicate inadequate levels of public services provided in some jurisdictions.

Overall, the school property tax rates are the major property tax element firms consider in their location decisions. Since school property tax rates comprise over 75% of the total property tax rates faced by a firm in Pennsylvania, the municipal property taxes are not an influential factor.

NONMANUFACTURING FIRM BIRTHS

Nonmanufacturing firm births were empirically examined using the same independent variables as manufacturing firm births, with the exception that market demand variables were added to the model.[5] Originally a regression was executed with population density (POPDEN) and per capita income (PCY) included. However, population density was highly correlated to several variables, leading to multicollinearity. [6] It was subsequently dropped from the model, leaving per capita income as the only extra variable for the nonmanufacturing estimations.

A methodology similar to that used for manufacturing firms is reported in the following two sections. First, the empirical results with only the average values as regressors are reported, followed by results for the model augmented with the ranges for the tax and expenditure variables.

Nonmanufacturing Firm Births and Average Tax Rates

The estimated coefficients and t-statistics using nonmanufacturing firm births as the dependent variable are listed in table 5.3.

TABLE 5.3 NONMANUFACTURING FIRM BIRTHS USING
AVERAGE VALUES
Dependent Variable BNOMAN76

Variable	Coefficient	T-Statistics	Signif. Level
CONSTANT	-1113.9390	-.991373	.3261841
SCHOOLAV	-131.2640	-2.449854	.117409#-01
INSTAVER	1.4608	1.016583	.3141507
MUNAVE74	33.7156	.943004	.3501247
POLFIR74	47.2253	4.883654	.1070492E-04
SANIT74	-20.4955	-1.968039	.5451184E-01
D2RATES	383.7030	2.663176	.1033232E-01
IHMILES	3.5996	1.182802	.2423724
AIRPORTS	177.3174	3.011179	.4041101E-02
CESTAB76	-46.5942	-2.014643	.4922937E-01
DUMMYMSA	56.6242	.311849	.7564268
CAPITLON	178.1364	.443853	.6590263
AVEWAG75	361.6360	1.931035	.5904614E-01
LANDPR74	.8915	2.912243	.5312516E-02
CAPRDFAC	796.3402	1.695288	.9611876E-01
PCY76	.2178	1.049753	.2987810

$R^2 = .893$ Degrees of Freedom = 51   Adjusted $R^2 = .862$

In regards to the fiscal variables, the results are very similar to those obtained for manufacturing firm births. The average school tax rate variable (SCHOOLAV) is negative and statistically significant at a level of .018. The signs of the coefficients of the other fiscal variables are the same as in the regression explaining manufacturing firm births. In addition, the variables that have high t-statistics for manufacturing firm births also have t-statistics greater than two in the nonmanufacturing regression. Therefore, the conclusions are similar. A two-tiered tax system and per capita police and fire expenditures are positively related to nonmanufacturing firm births, while high average school tax rates and per capita sanitation and sewage expenditures are negatively correlated.

More control variables are statistically significant for nonmanufacturing firm births. In addition to agglomeration effects, proxied by the number of airports in a county and high land prices, per capita research and development facilities are positively related to nonmanufacturing firm births. This is perplexing because R&D laboratories are generally believed to be used primarily by manufacturing firms. However, the statistical significance of this variable to the nonmanufacturing sector may be indicative of the agglomeration effects that give rise to the proximity of research and development facilities. Secondly, new manufacturing firms locating in a county are likely to be branch plants whose research and development activities are carried out a national corporate headquarters, and not necessarily close to the branch. In contrast, nonmanufacturing firms with R&D requirements would be more likely to look for closer local research facilities.

An interesting difference is that the coefficient of the average wage variable is both positive and statistically significant. One rationale is that since there is not a variable controlling for labor skills, high wages could indicate higher skills of the labor force. Another reason is that higher average wages could indicate higher incomes and purchasing power, thereby serving as a proxy for market demand potential in a county. Since nonmanufacturing firms are generally more dependent on local market demand, high average wages could be a positive factor in terms of both labor pool skills and potential consumer market demand.

The coefficient for per capita number of establishments is negative with a statistical significance level of .049. Therefore, nonmanufacturing firm births can be thwarted by a heavy concentration of firms per person in a locale. At first, this finding seems counter-intuitive. However, assuming the majority of nonmanufacturing firms are driven by local market demand potential, a saturation of firms in a county can lead to fierce competition for a finite set of local consumers. Therefore, it is logical that this variable is not statistically significant for manufacturing firms which are not dependent on local market demand conditions.

In summary, a large portion of the empirical results for nonmanufacturing firm births are very similar to those for the manufacturing regressand. High average school property tax rates and high per capita sanitation expenditures have a strong negative influence on nonmanufacturing firm births. High per capita police and fire expenditures, a two-tier property tax system and agglomeration economies are positive factors. However, in contrast to the manufacturing sector, research and development facilities and average wages are positively correlated with nonmanufacturing firm births, whereas the concentration of firms per person is negatively correlated. Local market demand potential may explain the positive coefficient for average wages as well as the negative coefficient for per capita number of establishments.

Nonmanufacturing Firm Births, Average Tax Rates and Ranges

The parameter estimates for nonmanufacturing firm births regressed against the average tax rates and the range of tax rates in a county are reported in table 5.4. As in the case of manufacturing firm births, this regression is the same as the preceding model, except that the variables SCHOODIF, INSTDIFF, and MUNDIFF have been added.

Compared to the regression for nonmanufacturing firm births using only average tax and expenditure variables, this regression offers additional information about how property tax rates affect the location decisions of nonmanufacturing firms. The hypothesis that property tax rate differentials only pertain to manufacturing location decisions because they are considered "footloose" can be rejected. High average school property tax rates have a statistically significant negative impact on nonmanufacturing firm births.[7] A wide range of school property tax rates (SCHOODIF), however, can lead to more nonmanufacturing firm births, just as is the case for manufacturing

TABLE 5.4 NONMANUFACTURING FIRM BIRTHS USING
AVERAGES AND RANGES
Dependent Variable BNOMAN76

Variable	Coefficient	T-Statistics	Signif. Level
CONSTANT	-1597.1850	-1.521098	.1347960
SCHOOLAV	-145.3142	-2.641101	.1111922E-01
SCHOODIF	57.2974	4.032533	.1966563E-03
INSTAVER	2.0772	1.571401	.1226588
INSTDIFF	-1.8869	-2.183475	.3392126E-01
MUNAVE74	24.1325	.655361	.5153640
MUNDIF74	-27.9138	-1.144310	.2581693
POLFIR74	46.5923	5.949425	.2995049E-06
SANIT74	-18.4109	-1.869124	.6771337E-01
D2RATES	406.2745	2.898890	.5631020E-02
IHMILES	3.5273	1.173284	.2464712
AIRPORTS	190.5418	3.679265	.5910355E-03
CAPITLON	59.3657	.165465	.8692731
AVEWAG75	402.7740	2.015406	.4948011E-01
CESTAB76	-51.9163	-2.179088	.3426503E-01
LANDPR74	.5959	2.616397	.3568240E-01
CAPRDFAC	801.6164	1.605399	.1149659
DUMMYMSA	83.1160	.480378	.6331411
PCY76	.3402	1.706404	.9439585E-01

$R^2 = .909$ Degrees of Freedom = 48   Adjusted $R^2 = .876$

firm births. The t-statistic of this variable has a significance level of
.0002.

The two measures of instruction dollars per student (INSTAVER
and INSTDIFF) indicate that the amount of spending per pupil also
has a strong statistical relationship to nonmanufacturing firm births.
The average variable (INSTAVER) has a coefficient sign that is
positive, matching the results of the other three regressions. It has a
marginal level of significance of .12. The range between the largest
and smallest instructional spending per student is statistically
significant at a level of .034 for nonmanufacturing firm births. Just as
in the manufacturing firm birth regression, the sign of the coefficient
is negative, indicating that counties with wide disparities in the

amount of dollars spent per student have fewer nonmanufacturing firm births.

The findings related to the school tax rate variables (SCHOOLAV, SCHOODIF) and instruction dollars per student (INSTAVER, INSTDIFF) surprisingly match those for manufacturing firm births. Evidently nonmanufacturing firms are concerned with school tax rate differentials. They are attracted to counties with a large disparity in school taxes, but are repelled by those with a large disparity in instruction dollars spent per student. Perhaps they are locating in low school tax areas with close proximity to school districts with higher taxes to give their employees options for living in good school districts. These results seem to indicate that nonmanufacturing firms also desire variety in tax levels, but they prefer uniformity in instructional expenditures. Perhaps lower education expenditures affect the skill of the labor force. In addition, education expenditures may also be financed by state and federal aid, lowering property tax rates. In any case, at the school district interjurisdictional level, nonmanufacturing firms may be more "footloose" than previously believed. Empirical studies which only include the average values of these fiscal variables aggregated to county or state levels would miss this interesting finding.

Municipal tax rates do not appear to be important to nonmanufacturing firm location decisions. The variables MUNDIF74 and MUNAVE74 are not statistically significant. The statistical significance of the remaining fiscal variables are similar to those estimated in the other three regressions. A two-tier property tax system (D2RATES) and per capita police and fire expenditures (POLFIR74) are positively related to nonmanufacturing firm births. The coefficients have t-statistics with levels of significance of .006 and .0000003 respectively. Per capita sanitation expenditures are negatively correlated to nonmanufacturing firm births with a .068 level of statistical significance.

The control variables show the strong positive influence of airports and high land prices as proxies for agglomeration economies. Per capita research and development facilities are a marginally positive factor at a level of significance of .115. Once again, per capita number of firms has a negative relationship to the number of nonmanufacturing firm births in a county. The statistical significance is much stronger at a level of .03, than for the manufacturing sector. Potential market demand proxied by per capita income is a positive element to location decisions. The t-statistic has a statistical significance of .094. As in the case of the preceding regression, average wages are a positive and statistically significant element in nonmanufacturing firm location decisions.

MEASURING THE EFFECTS OF TAX RATE DIFFERENTIALS

The regression estimates of the augmented model for both manufacturing and nonmanufacturing firm births indicate that school property tax rates have a statistically significant influence on new firm location selections. An important consideration to policy makers is the size of the effect. The elasticity measures of the fiscal and control variables for both manufacturing and nonmanufacturing firms are shown in tables 5.6 and 5.7 at the end of the chapter.

The largest elasticities for the augmented models occur for the variables of the average school tax rates and the average instructional dollars per student. For example, a one per cent increase in the average school tax rate will lead to a 1.57% decrease in the number of manufacturing firm births and a 3.22% decrease in the number of nonmanufacturing firm births. The state average number of manufacturing firm births is 87.46 firms. Therefore, on average, a one per cent increase in the average school property tax rate would lead to 1.37 less manufacturing firm births per county. The average effect on nonmanufacturing firms, however, would be greater since the average number per county is higher. A one per cent increase in the average school property tax rate would lead to 31.9 less nonmanufacturing firm births per county.

A one per cent increase in spending on instruction per student can lead to a 1.3% increase in manufacturing firm births and a 1.44% increase in nonmanufacturing firm births. Using the state averages per county, this means 1.14 more manufacturing firms and 14.3 more nonmanufacturing firms would locate in a county with higher relative spending on instruction per student. The elasticities for the other fiscal variables are very small, so changes in those variables ultimately lead to negligible changes in the number of firm births in a county.

The elasticities of the control variables for manufacturing firms are inelastic. However, the elasticity measures of two control variables for nonmanufacturing firms are greater than one. Both per capita income and average wages are elastic, indicating that potential local market demand conditions are very important to nonmanufacturing firm location decisions.

CONCLUSION

In all four regressions, high average school property tax rates have a statistically significant negative impact on firm births in both the manufacturing and nonmanufacturing sectors of a local economy in the state of Pennsylvania. This finding lends additional support to the body of research which has indicated that tax differentials matter to locating firms. However, the results of the augmented model regressions indicate that a large variety of school property tax rates in a county can actually lead to more firm births in both sectors. This is a new and interesting finding not previously seen in the literature. The distribution of property tax rates is a statistically significant positive influence on new births.

High average municipal tax rates are not a detriment to local economic development. These variables have coefficients that are not statistically significant. Coupled with the positive correlation and importance of per capita police and fire expenditures, municipal taxes seem to be associated with a public goods argument. Firms are willing to pay municipal taxes in return for the benefits of public goods and services they finance.

Other positive factors are primarily derived from a county having cities with a two-tier property tax system and agglomeration economies as evidenced by the statistical significance of airports and high land prices. Nonmanufacturing firm births are also very sensitive to local market demand potential, evidenced by the statistically significant and positive coefficients for per capita income and average wages. However, market saturation is a concern based on the negative and statistically significant coefficient of per capita number of business establishments.

In the following concluding chapter, the results of all the regressions are summarized in relationship to the original hypothesis stated in the chapter one. Based on the conclusions drawn from the results, a set of recommendations to policy makers is discussed. The chapter closes with a brief outline for areas of future research.

TABLE 5.5 REGRESSION RESULTS, BOTH SECTORS, BOTH MODELS[a]

Independent Variable	Manufac-turing	Manufacturing Augmented	Nonmanufac-turing	Nonmanu. Augmented
CONSTANT	-51.84	-71.04	-1113.94	-1597.18
	(-5.38)	(-.76)	(-.99)	(0.13)
SCHOOLAV	-5.38**	-6.25**	-131.26**	-145.31***
	(-2.09)	(-2.25)	(-2.45)	(-2.64)
SCHOODIF		6.05***		57.30***
		2.93		(4.03)
INSTAVER	0.11	0.17	1.46	2.08
	(0.81)	1.19	(1.02)	(1.57)
INSTDIFF		-0.22***		-1.89**
		(-2.83)		(-2.18)
MUNAVE74	0.58	-1.20	33.72	24.13
	(0.19)	(-0.34)	(0.94)	(0.66)
MUNDIF74		-1.79		-27.91
		(-0.80)		(-1.14)
POLFIR74	3.16***	3.20***	47.23***	46.59***
	(4.23)	5.53	(4.88)	(5.95)
SANIT74	-1.84**	-1.33	-20.50**	-18.41*
	(-2.26)	(-1.56)	(-1.97)	(-1.87)
D2RATES	20.58***	23.57***	383.70***	406.27***
	(2.92)	(3.55)	(2.66)	(2.90)
IHMILES	0.37	0.43	3.60	3.53
	(1.62)	(1.58)	(1.18)	(1.17)
AIRPORTS	23.63***	24.65***	177.32***	190.54***
	(4.19)	(4.89)	(3.01)	(3.68)
CESTAB76	-2.96	-3.54*	-46.59**	-51.92**
	(1.31)	(-1.66)	(-2.01)	(-2.18)
DUMMYMSA	5.66	7.70	56.62	83.11
	(0.31)	(0.46)	(0.31)	(0.48)
CAPITLON	24.70	7.41	178.14	59.37
	0.90	(0.28)	(0.44)	(0.17)
AVEWAG75	10.55	18.92	361.64*	402.77**
	(0.84)	(1.40)	(1.93)	(2.02)
LANDPR74	0.13***	0.19***	0.89***	0.60**
	(3.99)	(4.82)	(2.91)	(2.16)
CAPRDRAC	26.65	19.68	796.34*	801.61
	(0.87)	(0.53)	(1.70)	(1.61)
PCY76			0.22	0.34*
			(0.30)	(1.71)
R²	0.882	0.907	0.893	0.909
Adjusted R²	0.851	0.875	0.862	0.876
Degrees of Freedom	52	49	51	48

[a]Coefficient estimates are reported with t-statistics in parenthesis.
*Indicates significant at the 10% level.
**Indicates significant at the 5% level.
***Indicates significant at the 1% level.

Property Taxes & Local Development

TABLE 5.6 ELASTICITY MEASURES OF VARIABLES FOR MANUFACTURING FIRM BIRTHS

Model	Variable	Coefficient	Mean of X	Mean of Y	(C*(X/Y)) Elasticity Measure
Standard	SCHOOLAV	-5.38011	21.96	87.46	-1.35087
	INSTAVER	0.11047	686.11	87.46	0.86663
	MUNAVE74	0.57566	7.3844	87.46	0.04860
	POLFIR74	3.16322	15.33	87.46	0.55445
	SANIT74	-1.83723	9.71	87.46	-0.20397
	D2RATES	20.57598	0.3280	87.46	0.07716
	IHMILES	0.36569	24.48	87.46	0.10236
	AIRPORTS	23.62756	1.69	87.46	0.45656
	CESTAB76	-2.95841	18.34	87.46	-0.62037
	CAPITLON	24.69652	0.0002	87.46	0.00005
	AVEWAG75	10.54506	4.39	87.46	0.52930
	LANDPR74	0.12525	732.64	87.46	1.04924
	CAPRDFAC	26.65140	0.0001	87.46	0.00002
Augmented	SCHOOLAV	-6.25115	21.96	87.46	-1.56958
	SCHOODIF	6.05094	6.8761	87.46	0.47572
	INSTAVER	0.16603	686.11	87.46	1.30248
	INSTDIFF	-0.21753	154.48	87.46	-0.38422
	MUNAVE74	-1.20087	7.3844	87.46	0.10139
	MUNDIF74	-1.78759	8.6388	87.46	-0.17657
	POLFIR74	3.19534	15.33	87.46	0.56008
	SANIT74	-1.32862	9.71	87.46	-0.14751
	D2RATES	23.56757	0.32797	87.46	0.08838
	IHMILES	0.42594	24.48	87.46	0.11922
	AIRPORTS	24.65026	1.69	87.46	0.47632
	CESTAB76	-3.53870	18.34	87.46	-0.74205
	CAPITLON	7.40873	0.0002	87.46	0.00002
	AVEWAG75	18.91951	4.39	87.46	0.94965
	LANDPR74	40.10874	732.64	87.46	0.91088
	CAPRDFAC	19.67793	0.0001	87.46	0.00001

TABLE 5.7 ELASTICITY MEASURES OF
VARIABLES FOR NONMANUFACTURING FIRM BIRTHS

Model	Variable	Coefficient	Mean of X	Mean of Y	(C*(X/Y)) Elasticity Measure
Standard	SCHOOLAV	131.2640	21.96	990.54	-2.91009
	INSTAVER	1.4608	686.11	990.54	1.01181
	MUNAVE74	33.7156	7.3844	990.54	0.25135
	POLFIR74	47.2253	15.33	990.54	0.73088
	SANIT74	-20.4955	9.71	990.54	-0.20091
	D2RATES	383.7030	0.3280	990.54	0.12704
	IHMILES	3.5996	24.48	990.54	0.08896
	AIRPORTS	177.3174	1.69	990.54	0.30253
	CESTAB76	-46.5942	18.34	990.54	-0.86270
	CAPITLON	178.1364	0.0002	990.54	0.00003
	AVEWAG75	361.6360	4.39	990.54	1.60274
	LANDPR74	0.8915	732.64	990.54	0.65938
	CAPRDFAC	796.3402	0.0001	990.54	0.00005
	PCY76	0.2178	5590.49	990.54	1.22931
Augmented	SCHOOLAV	-145.3142	21.96	990.54	-3.22158
	SCHOODIF	57.2974	6.8761	990.54	0.39775
	INSTAVER	2.0772	686.11	990.54	1.43877
	INSTDIFF	-1.8869	154.48	990.54	-0.29428
	MUNAVE74	24.1325	7.3844	990.54	0.17991
	MUNDIF74	-27.9138	8.6388	990.54	-0.24344
	POLFIR74	46.5922	15.33	990.54	0.72108
	SANIT74	-18.4109	9.71	990.54	-0.18048
	D2RATES	406.2745	0.3280	990.54	0.13452
	IHMILES	3.5273	24.48	990.54	0.08717
	AIRPORTS	190.5418	1.69	990.54	0.32509
	CAPITLON	59.3657	0.0002	990.54	0.00001
	AVEWAG75	402.7740	4.39	990.54	1.78506
	CESTAB76	-51.9163	18.34	990.54	-0.96124
	LANDPR74	0.5959	732.64	990.54	0.44075
	CAPRDFAC	801.6164	0.0001	990.54	0.00005
	PCY76	0.3402	5590.49	990.54	1.92014

NOTES

1. All four specifications were first estimated using Ordinary Least Squares (OLS). They were re-estimated using the White procedure to correct for heteroscedasticity. In all instances, the t-statistics improved using the White procedure. Therefore all the results reported are those obtained using Generalized Least Squares (GLS).

2. Walter Rybeck, "Pennsylvania Experiments in Property Tax Modernization," *NTA Forum* (Spr. 1991): 3.

3. Leslie E. Papke, "Subnational Taxation and Capital Mobility: Estimates of Tax-Price Elasticities," *National Tax Journal* 49, no. 2 (1987): 195.

4. Refer to page 51 for further detail.

5. Refer to page 44 in chapter three for an outline of the augmented model.

6. The correlation coefficients were .84 with police and fire expenditures and .63 with average instruction dollars per student.

7. The significance level is .011.

VI

Conclusion

Local governments are highly dependent on property taxes as a source of revenue. A sluggish or shrinking local economy can lead to an eroding tax base while expenditures for public services either remain the same, or increase if social problems such as poverty or an obsolete infrastructure drain the coffers. New businesses help local economies not only by providing more employment, but also by increasing the tax base. Therefore, local policy makers are concerned with how property tax rates affect the number of new businesses locating within their jurisdictions. If high property tax rates relative to neighboring locales "drive industry out," then it is in the best interest of local governments to curb tax rate increases. Local policy makers are faced with the question of whether or not property tax rate differentials affect local economic development. To date, the answer has not been settled by the empirical work reviewed in chapter two.

This study is another attempt to focus on how property tax rates influence firm births. It is the only study that investigates the separate effects of the different property tax rates faced by a firm locating into a county. Other empirical studies aggregate school and municipal property taxes, and many average them into other state or local government taxes. This study also investigates how the disparity or range of property tax rates in a county may affect the location decisions of new firms.

THE NULL HYPOTHESIS

The null hypothesis that property tax rate differentials are not an important factor in location decisions of new firms can be rejected with certain qualifications. First, high relative school property tax rates have a negative effect not only on "footloose" manufacturing firm births, but also on nonmanufacturing firm births as well. Secondly, counties with a diversity of property tax rates charged by school districts have a greater propensity to attract new business establishments than those counties with more homogeneous school property tax rates. Counties which offer a menu of choices of different school district tax packages may enable cost conscious firms to locate in a low tax rate school district and enjoy the positive external benefits provided by neighboring higher tax rate school districts.

Thirdly, municipal property tax rates, that is, those levied by the local municipality and the county, do not have strong statistical importance to location decisions for "footloose" manufacturing firms, nor for nonmanufacturing firm births. Since the per capita police and fire expenditures variable measuring the level of public services offered by municipalities has a statistically significant and positive coefficient, it is possible that firms view municipal taxes as payment for publicly provided goods and services.

Finally, the results of the regression estimates indicate that a two-tier property tax system can have a positive influence on the location of firms in a county. Therefore, property tax rate differentials can be a statistically significant element in location decisions.

MEASURING THE EFFECTS OF TAX RATE DIFFERENTIALS

The largest elasticities of the fiscal variables for the augmented models occur for average school tax rates and the average instructional dollars spent per student. This is not surprising since school property tax rates are the largest percentage of the total property tax rates faced by a firm. Based on the elasticities calculated in the previous chapter, a one per cent increase in the average school property tax rate would lead to 1.37 less manufacturing firm births per county and 31.9 less nonmanufacturing firm births per county.[1]

A one per cent increase in spending on instruction per student can lead to an average of 1.14 more manufacturing firms and 14.3 more nonmanufacturing firms locating in a county.[2] The elasticities for the other fiscal variables are very small, so changes in those variables ultimately lead to negligible changes in the number of firm births in a county.

POLICY RECOMMENDATIONS

The findings of this study indicate that policy makers concerned about the impact of tax differentials on local economic development should use caution in raising school property tax rates without offsetting those increases with additional education spending on instruction. For manufacturing firms, the offset is nearly complete, so the net effect of both increases does not adversely impact manufacturing firm location decisions. However, there will be a net loss of nonmanufacturing firms, since they seem to be more sensitive to the tax rate increase than to the additional spending on educational instruction. On average the net loss would be 17.6 nonmanufacturing firm births in a county.

Municipal property tax rate increases do not seem to have major impacts on location decisions of firms in both sectors. However, a two-tier property tax system appears to have a positive influence on firm births in both sectors. Agglomeration economies seem to be the predominate factor in the nonfiscal elements analyzed. However, it is unlikely that sparsely populated, rural counties would have the ability to decrease their average school property taxes sufficiently to compensate for the absence of agglomeration economies. The tax elasticities are not large enough.

CONCLUSION

The results of this study lend support to the body of literature which has found that tax differentials can affect the location decisions of business establishments. However, the augmented model regressions also uncovered another aspect. The distribution of property tax rates in a county can affect the number of new firms locating in it. A large disparity in the tax rates charged by school districts can have a positive influence on the number of firm births. One area for future investigation is what makes the distribution of tax rates have high explanatory power.

The biggest surprise in the results of this study is the statistical significance of the fiscal variables in the nonmanufacturing sector. General location theory stipulates that only "footloose" or manufacturing firms will gravitate to low tax jurisdictions, while nonmanufacturing firms will locate close to where their consumer base resides, regardless of tax rate differentials. Since the data base contains a large enough sample size of nonmanufacturing firms classified by industry, future research should investigate the sensitivity of location decisions of firms in different industries to property tax rate differentials. Perhaps a large portion of nonmanufacturing firms are more "footloose" than traditionally believed.

As long as the federalism inherent in our government structure is maintained, it is possible that an array of local municipalities offering different tax-expenditure budgets can induce businesses, as well as residents, "to vote with their feet." Whether or not businesses choose sites with fiscal factors at the forefront of their location criterion is still subject to debate and empirical analysis.

NOTES

1. The elasticities are -1.57 for manufacturing and -3.22 for nonmanufacturing.

2. The elasticities are 1.14 for manufacturing and 1.13 for nonmanufacturing.

Bibliography

Acs, Zoltan J. and David B. Audretsch. "Births and Firm Size."*Southern Economic Journal* 56, no. 2 (October 1989): 467-475.

Advisory Commission on Intergovernmental Relations (ACIR). *Fiscal Balance in the American Federal System.* Vol. 2, Metropolitan Fiscal Disparities. Report A31. Washington, D.C.: The commission, 1967.

————. *State-Local Taxation and Industrial Location.* Report A-30. Washington, D.C.: The commission, 1967.

Allen, Ralph C. and Jack H. Stone. "The Locational Criteria of Footloose Firms: A Formal Model." *The Review of Regional Studies* 19, no. 2 (Spring 1989): 3-17.

Bartik, Timothy J. "Business Location Decisions in the United States: Estimates of the Effects of Unionization, Taxes, and Other Characteristics of States." *Journal of Business and Economic Statistics* 3, no. 1 (January 1985): 14-22.

————. "The Effects of Property Taxes and Other Local Public Policies on the Intrametropolitan Pattern of Business Location." In *Industry Location and Public Policy*, edited by Henry Herzog and Alan Schlottmann, 57-80. Knoxville, TN: Univ.of Tennessee Press, 1991.

————. "The Effects of State and Local Taxes On Economic Development: A Review of Recent Research." *Economic Development Quarterly* 6, no. 1 (February 1992): 102-110.

————. "Small Business Start-Ups in the United States: Estimates of the Effects of Characteristics of States." *Southern Economic Journal* 55, no. 4 (April 1989): 1004-1018.

————. "Small Business Start-Ups in the United States: Estimates of the Effects of Characteristics of States." Vanderbilt Univ., Working Paper no. 87-W15, June 1987.

————. "Taxes and Local Economic Development: What Do We Know and What Can We Know?" In *Proceedings of the Eighty-Seventh Annual Conference on Taxation*, held by the National Tax Association-Tax Institute of America, Charleston, S.C., November 13-15, 1994 (1995):102-106.

————. *Who Benefits from State and Local Economic Development Policies?* Kalamazoo, Michigan: W.E. Upjohn Institute for Employment Research, 1991.

Beck, John H. "Tax Competition, Uniform Assessment, and the Benefit Principle." *Journal of Urban Economics* 13 (1983): 127-146.

Benson, B.L. and R.N. Johnson. "The Lagged Impact of State and Local Taxes on Economic Activity and Political Behavior." *Economic Inquiry* 24, no. 2 (July 1986): 389-401.

Birch, David L. *Job Creation in America*. NY: The Free Press, 1987.

————. "The Job Generation Process." Working Paper published by the M.I.T. Program on Neighborhood and Regional Change, Cambridge, Mass., 1979.

Birch, David L., et al. "The Behavioral Foundation of Neighborhood Change." Department of Housing and Urban Development, Jan. 1979.

Blair, John P. and Robert Premus. "Major Factors in Industrial Location: A Review." *Economic Development Quarterly* 1, no. 1 (February 1987): 72-85.

Bloom, C.C. *State and Local Tax Differentials.* Iowa City: Bureau of Business Research, State Univ. of Iowa, 1955.

Bowman, John H. and John L. Mikesell. "Elected Versus Appointed Assessors and the Achievement of Assessment Uniformity." *National Tax Journal* 42, no. 2 (June 1989): 181-189.

Bradbury, Katharine L. and Helen F. Ladd. "Changes in the Revenue Raising Capacity of US Cities, 1970-1982." *New England Economic Review* (March/April 1985): 20-37.

Campbell, A.K. "Taxes and Industrial Location in the New York Metropolitan Region." *National Tax Journal* 11 (September 1958).

Canto, Victor A. and Robert J. Webb. "The Effect of State Fiscal Policy on State Relative Economic Performance." *Southern Economic Journal* 54, no. 1 (July 1987): 186-202.

Carlton, Dennis W. "The Location and Employment Choices of New Firms: An Econometric Model with Discrete and Continuous Endogenous Variables." *The Review of Economics and Statistics* (August 1983): 440-449.

————. "Why New Firms Locate Where They Do: An Econometric Model." In *Interregional Movements and Regional Growth*, edited by William C. Wheaton, 13-50. Washington, DC: Urban Institute, 1979.

Carroll, Robert and Michael Wasylenko. "Do State Business Climates Matter?—Evidence of a Structural Change." *National Tax Journal* 42, no. 1 (March 1994): 19-37.

————. "The Shifting Fate of Fiscal Variables and their Effect on Economic Development." *National Tax Association-Tax Institute of America Proceedings of the 82nd Annual Conference* (1989): 283-290.

Chalmers, James A. and Terrance L. Beckhelm. "Shift and Share and the Theory of Industrial Location." *Regional Studies* 10 (1976): 15-23.

Charney, Alberta H. "Intraurban Manufacturing Location Decisions and Local Tax Differentials." *Journal of Urban Economics* 14 (1983): 184-205.

Church, Albert M. "The Effects of Local Government Expenditure and Property Taxes on Investment." *Journal of the American Real Estate & Urban Economics Association* 9 (1984): 165-180.

Commonwealth of Pennsylvani Tax Study Committee. *The Tax Problem.* Philadelphia, 1953.

Coughlin, Cletus C., Joseph V.Terza, and Vachira Arromdee. "State Characteristics and the Location of Foreign Direct Investment within the United States." *Review of Economics and Statistics* (1991): 675-683.

Courant, Paul N. "How Would You Know a Good Economic Development Policy if You Tripped Over One? Hint: Don't Just Count Jobs." *National Tax Journal* 47, no. 4 (December 1994): 863-881.

Crihfield, John B. "A Structural Empirical Analysis of Metropolitan Labor Demand." *Journal of Regional Science* 29, no. 3 (1989): 347-371.

————. "Manufacturing Supply: A Long-Run, Metropolitan View," *Regional Science and Urban Economics* 20 (1990): 327-349.

Deich, Michael. "State Taxes and Manufacturing Plant Location." *National Tax Association-Tax Institute of America Proceedings of the 82nd Annual Conference* (1989): 290-299.

Due, John F. "Studies of State-Local Tax Influences on Location of Industry." *National Tax Journal* (June 1961): 163-173.

Duffy, Neal E. "The Determinants of State Manufacturing Growth Rates: A Two-Digit-Level Analysis." *Journal of Regional Science* 34, no. 2 (1994): 137-162.

Ebel, Robert D. and James Ortbal. "Direct Residential Property Tax Relief." *Intergovernmental Perspective* 15, No. 2 (Spring 1989): 9-14.

Eberts, Randall W. "Some Empirical Evidence on the Linkage between Public Infrastructure and Local Economic Development." In *Industry Location and Public Policy*, edited by Henry Herzog and Alan Schlottmann, 83-96. Knoxville, TN: Univ. of Tennessee Press, 1991.

Epple, Dennis and Allan Zelenitz. "The Implications of Competition Among Jurisdictions: Does Tiebout Need Politics?" *Journal of Political Economy* 8, no. 6 (1981): 1197-1217.

Erickson, Rodney A. "Corporations, Branch Plants, and Employment Stability in Nonmetropolitan Areas." In *Industrial Location and Regional Systems*, edited by John Rees et al., 135-153. NY: J. F. Bergin Pub. Inc., 1981.

Erickson, Rodney A. and Michael Wasylenko. "Firm Relocation and Site Selection in Suburban Municipalities." *Journal of Urban Economics* 8 (1980): 69-85.

Fischel, William A. "Fiscal and Environmental Considerations in the Location of Firms in Suburban Communities." Ph.D. dissertation, Princeton Univ., 1974.

———. "Fiscal and Environmental Considerations in the Location of Firms in Suburban Communities." In *Fiscal Zoning and Land-Use Controls*, edited by E. S. Mills and W. E. Oates, 119-174. Mass: Lexington Books, 1975.

Floyd, J.S. *Effects of Taxation on Industrial Location.* Chapel Hill: Univ. of N. Carolina Press, 1952.

Fox, William F. "Fiscal Differentials and Industrial Location: Some Empirical Evidence." *Urban Studies* 18 (1981): 105-111.

—————. "Local Taxes and Industrial Location." *Public Finance Quarterly* 6 (1978): 93-114.

—————. "Property Tax Influences on Industrial Location Within a Metropolitan Area: A report for the Department of Economics and Community Development." Columbus: State of Ohio, 1973.

Fox, William F. and Matthew N. Murray. "Local Public Policies and Interregional Business Development." *Southern Economic Journal* 57, no. 2 (Oct. 1990): 413-427.

Friedman, Joseph, Daniel A. Gerlowski and Johnathan Silberman. "What Attracts Foreign Multinational Corporations? Evidence from Branch Plant Location in the United States." *Journal of Regional Science* 32, no. 4 (November 1992): 403-418.

Genetski, Robert J. and Young D. Chin. "The Impact of State and Local Taxes on Economic Growth." Chicago: Harris Economic Research Office Service, no. 3, 1978.

Goldberg, Michael A. "An Economic Model of Intrametropolitan Industrial Location." *Journal of Regional Science* 10, no. 1 (1970): 75-79.

Greenhut, M.L. *Plant Location in Theory and Practice: The Economics of Space.* Chapel Hill: Univ. of N. Carolina Press, 1956.

Grieson, Ronald E. et al. "The Effect of Business Taxation on the Location of Industry." *Journal of Urban Economics* 4 (1977): 170-185.

Gudgin, Graham. *Industrial Location Processes and Regional Employment Growth.* England: Saxon House, 1979.

Gyourko, Joseph. "Effects of Local Tax Structures on the Factor Intensity Composition of Manufacturing Activity Across Cities." *Journal of Urban Economics* 22 (1987): 151-164.

———. "New Firm Activity and Employment Changes amoung the Localities in the Philadelphia Area, 1980-1983." In *Economic Development Within the Philadelphia Metropolitan Area,* edited by Anita A. Summers and Thomas F. Luce, 51-60. Philadelphia: Univ. of Pennsylvania Press, 1987.

Gyourko, Joseph and Joseph Tracy. "On the Political Economy of Land Value Capitalization and Local Public Sector Rent Seeking In a Tiebout Model." *Journal of Urban Economics* 26 (1989): 152-173.

Hamilton, Bruce. "A Review: Is the Property Tax a Benefit Tax?" In *Local Provision of Public Services: The Tiebout Model After Twenty-five Years,* edited by G.R. Zodrow, 85-107. New York: Academic Press, 1983.

Harrison, Bennett and Sandra Kanter. "The Political Economy of States' Job-Creation Business Incentives." *American Institute of Planners* 44, no. 4 (Oct. 1978): 424-435.

Helms, L. Jay. "The Effect of State and Local Taxes on Economic Growth: A Time Series-Cross Section Approach." *Review of Economics and Statistics* (Nov. 1985): 574-582.

Hodge, J. H. "A Study of Regional Investment Decisions." In *Research in Urban Economics,* edited by J. V. Henderson, Vol. 1. Greenwich CT: JAI Press, 1981.

Hotelling, H. "Stability in Competition." *Economic Journal* 39 (1929): 41-57.

Howland, Marie. "Property Taxes and the Birth and Intraregional Location of New Firms." *Journal of Planning, Education and Research* 4 (1985): 148-156.

Ihlanfeldt, D. R. and Michael D. Raper. "The Intrametropolitan Location of New Office Firms." *Land Economics* 66, no. 2 (May 1990): 182-198.

Johnson, K. P., J. R. Kort and H. L. Friedenberg. "Regional and State Projections of Income, Employment, and Population to the Year 2000." *Survey of Current Business* 70, no. 5 (May 1990): 33-54.

Jones, Bryan D. "Public Policies and Economic Growth in the American States." *Journal of Politics* 52, no. 1 (February 1990): 219-233.

Kieschnick, Michael. *Taxes and Growth*. Wash. D.C.: Council of State Planning Agencies, 1981.

————. "Venture Capital and Urban Development." In *Financing State and Local Economic Development*, edited by Michael Barker, 305-358. Durham, N.C.: Duke Press Policy Studies, 1983.

Klaassen, L. H. and W. T. M. Molle, editors. *Industrial Mobility and Migration in the European Community*. Great Britain: Gower Pub. Co. Ltd., 1983.

Ladd, Helen F. and Katharine L. Bradbury. "City Taxes and Property Tax Bases." *National Tax Journal* (Dec. 1988): 503-523.

Losch, A. *The Economics of Location*, translated by W. H. Woglom from *Die Raumliche Ordung der Wirtscdft* published in 1940. New Haven: Yale Univ. Press, 1954.

Luce, Thomas F., Jr. "The Determinants of Metropolitan Area Growth Disparities in High-Technology and Low-Technology Industries." Working Paper. Department of Public Administration, Pennsylvania State Univ., 1990.

————. "Local Taxes, Public Services and Intrametropolitan Location of Firms and Households." *Public Finance Quarterly* 22, no. 2 (April 1994): 139-67.

Luce, Thomas F. and Anita A. Summers. *Local Fiscal Issues in the Philadelphia Metropolitan Area.* Philadelphia: Univ. of Pennsylvania Press, 1987.

Malecki, Edward J. "Recent Trends in Location of Industrial Research & Development: Regional Development Implications for the United States." In *Industrial Location and Regional Systems*, edited by John Rees, et al. NY: J.F. Bergin Pub. Inc., 1981.

McConnell, Virginia D. and Robert M. Schwab. "The Impact of Environmental Regulation of Industry Location Decisions: The Motor Vehicle Industry." *Land Economics* 66, no. 1 (February 1990): 67-81.

McDonald, John F. "Local Property Tax Differences and Business Real Estate Values." *Journal of Real Estate Finance and Economics* 6 (1993): 277-287.

McGuire, Therese. "The Effect of New Firm Locations on Local Property Taxes." *Journal of Urban Economics* 22 (Oct. 1987): 223-229.

————."Essays on Firm Location in a Metropolitan Area." Ph.D. Dissertation, Princeton Univ., 1983.

————. "Interstate Tax Differentials, Tax Competition, and Tax Policy." *National Tax Journal* 39 (Sept. 1986): 367-73.

McHone, W. Warren. "Supply-Side Considerations in the Location of Industry in Suburban Communities: Empirical Evidence from the Philadelphia SMSA." *Land Economics* 62, no. 1 (February 1986): 64-73.

McLure, Charles E. "The Interstate Exporting of State and Local Taxes: Estimates for 1962." *National Tax Journal* 20 (1967): 49-77.

————. "The 'New View' of the Property Tax: A Caveat." *National Tax Journal* 30 (1977): 69-75.

McMillan, Melville L. "On Measuring Congestion of Local Public Goods." *Journal of Urban Economics* 26 (1989): 131-137.

McNertney, Edward M. "The Effect of State and Local Taxation on the Location of Industrial Employment." *The New England Journal of Business and Economics* 6, no. 2 (Spring 1980): 13-22.

Mieszkowski, Peter. "Effects of Business Taxation: The Special Case of Small Business." In *The Vital Majority: Small Business in the American Economy*, edited by Dean Carson, 449-467. Wash. D.C.: Small Business Administration, 1973.

————. "The Property Tax: An Excise Tax or a Profits Tax?" *Journal of Public Economics* 1 (1972): 73-93.

Miller, E. Williard. "Spatial Organization of Manufacturing in Nonmetropolitan Pennsylvania." In *Industrial Location and Regional Systems*, edited by John Rees et al., 155-169. NY: J.F. Bergin Pub. Inc., 1981.

Mills, Edwin S. and Wallace E. Oates. *Fiscal Zoning and Land Use Controls*. Mass: Lexington Books, 1975.

Misiolek, Walter S. and Harold W. Elder. "The Influence of State Tax Structures on State Economic Growth." Unpublished paper, The Univ. of Alabama, Oct. 1989.

Mofidi, Alaeddin and Joe A. Stone, "Do State and Local Taxes Affect Economic Growth?" *The Review of Economics and Statistics* 72, no. 4 (Nov. 1990): 686-691.

Morgan, Willaim E. "The Effects of State and Local Tax and Financial Inducements on Industrial Location." Ph.D. Dissertation, Univ. of Colorado, 1964.

Moriarty, Barry M., et al. *Industrial Location and Community Development.* Chapel Hill: Univ. of NC Press, 1980.

Mullen, John K. "Property Tax Exemptions and Local Fiscal Stress." *National Tax Journal* 43, no. 4 (Dec. 1990): 467-479.

Munnell, Alicia H. "How Does Public Infrastructure Affect Regional Economicperformance?" *New England Economic Review* (Sept/Oct 1990): 11-33.

Murray, Matthew N. "Using State Policies to Promote Economic Development." In *Proceedings of the Eighty-Sixth Annual Conference on Taxation,* held by the National Tax Association-Tax Institute of America, St. Paul, Minnesota, November 7-10, 1993 (1994):158-163.

Newman, Robert J. and Dennis H. Sullivan. "Econometric Analysis of Business Tax Impacts on Industrial Location: What Do We Know, and How Do We Know It?" *Journal of Urban Economics* 23 (March 1988): 214-234.

Norman, George. *Economies of Scale, Transport Costs, and Location.* Boston: Martinus Nijhoff Pub., 1979.

Oakland, William H. "Local Taxes and Intraurban Industrial Location: A Survey." In *Metropolitan Financing and Growth Management Policies,* edited by F.F. Break, 13-30. Madison: Univ. of Wisconsin Press, 1978.

Oates, Wallace E. "The Effects of Property Taxes and Local Public Spending on Property Values: An Empirical Study of Tax Capitalization and the Tiebout Hypothesis." *Journal of Political Economy* 77, no. 6 (Nov/Dec 1969): 1004-08.

O'hUallachain, Breandan O. and Mark A. Satterthwaite. "Sectoral Growth Patterns at the Metropolitan Level: An Evaluation of economic Development Incentives." *Journal of Urban Economics* 31, (1992): 25-58.

Papke, James A. and Leslie E. Papke. "Measuring Differential State-Local Tax Liabilities and their Implications for Business Investment Location." *National Tax Journal* (Sept. 1986): 357-66.

Papke, Leslie. "Interstate Business Tax Differentials and New Firm Location." *Journal of Public Economics* 45, no. 1 (June 1991): 47-68.

———. "The Location of New Manufacturing Plants and State Business Taxes." *Proceedings of the 79th Annual Conference of the National Tax Association* (Nov. 1986): 44-55.

———. "The Responsiveness of Industrial Activity to Interstate Tax Differentials: A Comparison of Elasticities." In *Industry Location and Public Policy*, edited by Henry Herzog and Alan Schlottmann, 120-134. Knoxville, TN: Univ. of Tennessee Press, 1991.

———. "Subnational Taxation and Capital Mobility: Estimate of Tax-Price Elasticities." *National Tax Journal* 40, no. 2 (1987): 191-203.

———. "Taxes and Other Determinants of Gross State Product in Manufacturing: A First Look." *National Tax Association-Tax Institute of American Proceedings of the 82nd Annual Conference* (1989): 274-282.

Parai, Amar K. and John H. Beck. "The Incidence of Classified Property Taxes in a Three-Sector Model with an Imperfectly Mobile Population." *Journal of Urban Economics* 25 (Jan. 1989): 77-92.

Peddle, Michael T. "The Appropriate Estimation of Intrametropolitan Firm Location Models: An Empirical Note." *Land Economics* 63 (Aug. 1987): 303-305.

Plaut, Thomas R. and Joseph E. Pluta. "Business Climate, Taxes and Expenditures and State Industrial Growth in the United States." *Southern Economic Journal* (July 1983): 99-119.

Quan, N.T. and J.H. Beck. "Public Education Expenditures and State Economic Growth: Northeast and Sunbelt Regions." *Southern Economic Journal* 54, no. 1 (July 1987): 361-376.

Rees, John, Geoffrey J.S. Hewings and Howard A. Stafford, editors. *Industrial Location and Regional Systems.* NY: J.F. Bergin Pub, Inc., 1981.

Reynolds, Paul. "Autonomous Firm Dynamics and Economic Growth in the United States, 1986-1990." *Regional Studies* 28, no. 4 (July 1994): 429-442.

Romans, Thomas and Ganti Subrahmanyam. "State and Local Taxes, Transfers and Regional Economic Growth." *Southern Economic Journal* 46 (1979): 435-44.

Rosen, Harvey S. and David J. Fullerton. "A Note on Local Tax Rates, Public Benefit Levels, and Property Values." *Journal of Political Economy* 85, no. 21 (1977): 433-440.

Rybeck, Walter. "Pennsylvania Experiments in Property Tax Modernization." *NTA Forum* (Spring 1991): 1-5.

Sander, William. "Local Taxes, Schooling, and Jobs in Illinois." Office of Real Estate Research Paper No. 75, College of Commerce and Business Administration, Univ. of Illinois at Urbana-Champaign, December 1989.

Schmenner, Roger W. "City Taxes and Industry Location." Ph.D. dissertation, Yale University, 1973.

————."City Taxes and Industry Location." *1973 Proceedings National Tax Association-Tax Institute of America.* Columbus Ohio: NTA-TIA, 1974.

————. "City Taxes and Industry Location." Yale University Mimeo, 1975.

————. *Making Business Location Decisions.* NJ: Prentice-Hall, Inc., 1982.

————. "The Manufacturing Location Decision: Evidence from Cincinnati and New England." Economic Development Research Report, 1978.

Schmenner, R. W., J. Huber and R. Cook. "Geographic Differences and the Location of New Manufacturing Facilities." *Journal of Urban Economics* 21, no. 1 (1987): 83-104.

Small, Kenneth A. *Geographically Differentiated Taxes and the Location of Firms.* Princeton, NJ: Princeton Urban & Regional Research Center, 1982.

Smith, Tim R. and William F. Fox. "Economic Development Programs for States in the 1990's." *Federal Reserve Bank of Kansas City Economic Review* (July/Aug. 1990): 25-35.

Sonstelie, Jon. "The Incidence of a Classified Property Tax." *Journal of Public Economics* 12 (1979): 75-85.

Stinson, Thomas F. *The Effects of Taxes and Public Finance Programs on Local Industrial Development: Agricultural Report 133.* Washington D.C.: Economic Research Service of the US Department of Agriculture, 1968.

Sullivan, Arthur M. "The General Equilibrium Effects of the Industrial Property Tax." *Regional Science and Urban Economics* 14 (1984): 547-563.

Tannenwald, Robert and Christine Kendrick. "Taxes and Capital Spending: Some New Evidence." In *Proceedings of the Eighty-Seventh Annual Conference on Taxation*, held by the National Tax Association-Tax Institute of America, Charleston, S.C., November 13-15, 1994 (1995): 113-121.

Testa, William A. "Metro Area Growth from 1976 to 1985: Theory and Evidence." Working Paper. Federal Reserve Bank of Chicago, January 1989.

Tiebout, Charles M. "A Pure Theory of Local Expenditures." *Journal of Political Economy* (October 1956): 416-424.

Thompson, W.R. and John M. Mattila. *An Econometric Model of Postwar State Industrial Development.* Detroit: Wayne State Univ. Press, 1959.

Townroe, P. M. *Industrial Movement.* Great Britain: SaxonHouse, 1979.

US Dept of Commerce. *1980 Census of Population: Characteristics of the Population* - Number of Inhabitants United States Summary. Chapter A, Part 1. PC80-1-A1. Bureau of the Census. April 1983, C3.223/5:980/A1 #159-C-52.

Wasylenko, Michael. "The Effect of Business Climate on Employment Growth." A report for the Minnesota Tax Study Commission, June 1984.

———. "Evidence of Fiscal Differentials and Intrametropolitan Firm Relocation." *Land Economics* 56, no. 3 (August 1980): 337-49.

———. "Has the Relationship Changed Between Taxes and Business Location Decisions?" In *Proceedings of the Eighty-Seventh Annual Conference on Taxation*, held by the National Tax Association-Tax Institute of America, Charleston, S.C., November 13-15, 1994 (1995):107-112.

————. "The Location of Firms: The Role of Taxes and Fiscal Incentives." In *Urban Government Finance*, edited by Roy Bahl, 155-190. Beverly Hills: Sage Publications, 1981.

Wasylenko, Michael and Therese McGuire. "Jobs and Taxes: The Effect of Business Climate on States' Employment Growth Rates." *National Tax Journal* 38, no. 4 (1985): 497-511.

Weber, A. *Alfred Weber's Theory of Location of Industries* translated by C. J. Friedrich from *Uber den Standord der Industrien* published in 1909. Chicago: Univ. of Chicago Press, 1929.

Wheaton, William C. "The Incidence of Inter-Jurisdictional Differences in Commercial Property Taxes." *National Tax Journal* 37 (1984): 515-28.

————. "Interstate Differences in the Level of Business Taxation." *National Tax Journal* 36 (March 1983): 83-94.

————. "The Impact of State Taxation on Life Insurance Growth." *National Tax Journal* 39 (March 1986): 85-95.

White, Michelle. "Firm Location in a Zoned Metropolitan Area." In *Fiscal Zoning and Land Use Controls*, edited. by E. S. Mills and W. E. Oates. Mass: Lexington Books, 1975.

————. "Property Taxes and Firm Location: Evidence from Proposition 13." In *Studies in State and Local Public Finance,* edited by Harvey Rosen, 83-107. Chicago: Chicago Univ. Press, 1986.

Woodward, Douglas P. "Locational Determinants of Japanese Manufacturing Start-Ups in the United States." *Southern Economic Journal* 58, no. 3 (January 1992): 690-708.

Yntema, D.B. *Michigan's Taxes on Business*. Holland, Michigan: Hope College, 1959.

Zodrow, George R. and Peter Mieszkowski. "The Incidence of the Property Tax: The Benefit View Versus the New View." In *Local Provision of Public Services: The Tiebout Model After Twenty-Five Years*, edited by G. R. Zodrow, 109-129. New York: Academic Press, 1983.

Index

3 1542 00168 6686

338.09748
K61p

DATE DUE

Trexler Library
Muhlenberg College
Allentown, PA 18104

DEMCO